Trust but Verify
A Great Injustice

Joyce M Stacks with Stuart Shockley

DEDICATION

For all who choose courage over cowardice and find justice

in the process ……… Joyce

For all you endured, I'd like to dedicate this to Diana and our

two children ……… Stuart

Contents

INTRODUCTION

When it came to détente, former President Reagan masterfully drew upon his talents as both a diplomat and a former actor in order to solidify his relationship with his political adversaries. One shining example relates to the negotiations leading up to the signing of the INF Treaty – the first treaty to actually reduce nuclear arms – on December 8, 1987 with his then counterpart, General Secretary, Mikhail Gorbachev. It was at that time President Reagan interjected a phrase adopted from a Russian proverb he'd learned from writer, Suzanne Massie, who had explained during the course of her tutelage regarding Russian culture, "Russians like to speak in proverbs."

Thus "Doveryai no proveryai" which translates to "Trust, but verify" became a signature phrase used frequently by Reagan, during the years between 1984 and 1987 whenever discussing U.S. relations with the Soviet Union.

Loosely interpreted, the phrase alluded to the extensive verification procedures both sides would require in order to monitor compliance with the treaty. Thus throughout their respective tenures in office, the men who answered the call to lead the world's two greatest super-powers during a time of peace were able to forge a relationship whose cornerstone was trust with one important caveat. As a result, citizens separated by far more than just language, but also cultural differences dating back to the beginning of the Cold War, each became co-beneficiaries of the same agreement.

But what happens when trust is no longer an option and your enemy is far more insidious by nature? Or when the people you learn you cannot trust turn out to be your own countrymen? It may have been Lord Byron who first coined the phrase, "Truth is stranger than fiction," back in 1823 with regard to the romantic pursuits of the legendary Don Juan, but in terms of subject matter, romance fails to adequately measure up in comparison to the resulting intrigue when one unsuspecting victim created a whole new computer programming language that would end up altering the way in which the world at large communicates as a whole. The resulting Molotov cocktail whose ingredients were one part high-level politics combined with corporate power and greed, not to mention one of the nation's best known security agencies have equated to systematic torture when it comes to the stealthy ruination of a man's life while simultaneously attempting to maintain the carefully crafted public images of those both directly and indirectly involved.

The following is a detailed account of the events perpetrated by all those individuals involved and spans the course of the past nineteen years. When I asked my potential client during the course of our first sit down about his motivation for wanting to tell his side of the story now – especially after the passage of so many years when there was only one year left on the original patent – the gentleman residing at the center of the controversy stated simply and succinctly, "Because there's no statute of limitations on malice," and I suppose that's true. I found it interesting that he perceived his life as having been ruined, while I on the other hand believed it may have just begun.

*PLEASE NOTE: This Story is based upon actual people and events that occurred in real time. Certain names and company information have either been changed or withheld in order to protect the innocent.

PREFACE

"All I wanted to do was to create something to make the world a better place," Stuart said, as he walked me out to my car in order to make certain there was no one around to bother me following our most recent interview.

"Maybe you did," I smiled back at him, in an effort to provide some degree of comfort where there had been little. I didn't know how a man goes about trying to reassemble his life once so much has been taken away from him. After all, recapturing time is a statistical impossibility; therefore, it would seem the most any of us could do under similar circumstances is to try and make sense out of what has happened to us and then summon the necessary effort in order to move forward as best we can.

I personally have never been much on the word closure, because when something affects us in such a profound manner, it marks us indelibly. Although life's battle scars may indeed fade over time, they're never really quite gone. Thus as I pulled out of the drive, I remember thinking how important it was to work toward giving him some measure of peace, if only to say, "I believe you, and you're not crazy."

Early on in our discussion, he had asked me, "Are you afraid?" which I suppose is a fair question considering he'd been systematically tortured by subtle means since 1989.

I replied, "No," and I meant that as far as I was concerned before going on with my explanation, "I'm just a simple storyteller. I certainly don't understand the technology, and I have no direct connection with any of those involved, therefore, I'm not in a position to hurt, weaken or threaten anybody. All I can really do is assist in giving you a voice."

"Then you still want to do this?" Stuart asked, and I answered, "Yes, but I do have one question as it relates to your motives …."

"What do you hope to gain?" It was only logical to assume that most people standing in his shoes might want some kind of retribution – justice if you will – that those who had sought to systematically destroy his life through extensive use of covert means might be forced to pay in much the same way he had, but his answer managed to surprise even me.

"I just want to be paid for my creation and then left alone to live out the balance of my life in peace."

I couldn't help thinking to myself, *good answer*. Then as I continued on my journey toward home, I thought about my own motives with the obvious one being because it's what I do, or at least what I attempt to do on some small scale. I write articles and stories based upon my own life's experiences in hope that the lessons I've learned might in some small way help others. I try not to focus so much on making a name for myself, but I do hope to make a living. However, helping Stuart might help me to achieve both.

I've always believed fate had a hand in the choices I've made, and as a result, I've tried to roll with life's many punches while always believing in the greater good, but this time it's not about me, but rather Stuart's story. In the end, I guess we're both kindred spirits whose lives have been brought together for a single-minded purpose. We don't ask for too much from the world, because in comparison to others, our needs are rather simple in nature, to have all we need and to be able to live life in peace.

1 GOD IS REAL

"I have to ask, why are you still alive? Why aren't you dead by now?"

Then without hesitation, Stuart answered, "Because God takes care of me."

I have to admit, it's endearing, if not more than just a little bit unusual these days to find someone - anyone - who is not already associated with the clergy, who is willing to stand solely upon faith, but he had his reason, and it deserves to be mentioned.

Back in 1964, Stuart's family relocated from Dallas to Hot Springs, Arkansas. Then when he was in the third grade, while playing outside with his brothers one day, he accidentally made direct contact with a live power line. As a result, he was hospitalized for 19 days in which he concluded *God was real*.

I've always maintained a certain theory about the people who suddenly find themselves in a sort of suspended-animation, otherwise known as that place between life and death. Those who manage to make their way back to the living are never quite the same as before. They are changed individuals, infused with intent to live life with purpose going forward. Their intuition tells them they have been given a rare gift and are therefore determined not to squander it. I believe Stuart is one such being.

Even at such a tender age, the fact he was cognoscente his life had somehow been spared more than likely played into his desire to make the world a better place. Therefore, after graduating high school, he went on to college where he eventually got married and began his family.

At Arkansas College of Technology, he discovered his niche in computer programming, though at first it gave him reason to pause. Instinctively, he recognized the power embedded within such technology. The only question remaining was whether or not such power would eventually take on the form of good or evil? Only time would tell. Nonetheless, he continued on his designated course and thus landed his first position as an IBM programmer at Ben Hogan Construction.

Fast-forwarding to May of 1994 – after 9 consecutive years of working as a computer programmer – Stuart and his family were finally enjoying the comfort afforded by a generous salary, paid insurance benefits and a growing savings account. By all appearances, life was good, but then old friends appeared …

2 BUILDING A RESUME'

"Let's talk about your work history … I mean where it all began, but I have to warn you, I'm not a technology guru, you'll have to explain things in the simplest of terms," I commented matter-of-factly, as I readied myself for taking notes.

At this point, I had already gained considerable insight as to what he'd been going through over the course of his professional career, and even though most people might find it difficult to digest in terms of believability, I'd known Stuart since we were children, and I knew when he was kidding and when I needed to take him seriously, not to mention I'd always had good intuition for identifying bullshit when I heard it. So at this point, all that was missing was the *why*.

*

He began, "In 1988, back at Computer *Data Services*, I invented an "A" auto-feed search program for collections of medical billing. I also created roll-screen processing and a system for online medical billing, which enabled transmitting and receiving with auto-posting to accounts."

"Can you elaborate in terms of what that means exactly?" I asked.

"Basically, I got tired of working with multiple operating systems. It was so labor-intensive, because no system was compatible with another. It was like English-speaking people trying to communicate in Chinese. I was worn out training new hires that would learn the job and then move on to another position elsewhere. So I guess you could say it all started with me trying to make my job easier," Stuart explained.

"But in the simplest terms, I created a new programming language that enabled one operating system to communicate with another seamlessly. I'd always liked figuring things like that out, it was fun for me," he continued.

"So what you had was *intellectual property*?" I asked. Met with a puzzled stare, I inquired further, "Are you familiar with that term?"

Then referring directly to myself, I went on, "I wasn't until someone I know quite well – an attorney – explained it to me several years ago.

"In a nutshell, it refers to creations of the mind … *such as inventions, designs, artistic works and other creations such as symbols, names and images used in commerce.*"

I'll admit it I had to use *Google* and a quick definition as provided by *Wiki* to help illustrate my point.

"Then yes," he agreed before going on to expand on the subject even further. "No one – not even *Microsoft* – was using roll screens at that time. I was the one who started that."

"Getting back to the story …." I prompted, knowing how easy it was to go off on tangents. I needed continuity to not only develop an understanding of everything that had occurred, but to be able to write about it as well.

"While still at Computer *Data Services*, I was asked to do an installation for my employer at a radiology clinic in Searcy, Arkansas, but the file I had saved, contained no records in it, and I couldn't restore it."

"Had somebody wiped it clean?" I asked.

"I couldn't possibly know that, but it was weird," Stuart replied before continuing.

"Then despite having a record year in earnings with the company, I was denied a raise at my annual review due to the mistake at Searcy. So I presented a print out of my time sheets containing all the money I had made for the company but still failed to receive a raise.

"So I ended up sending out resumes' to

other companies as a result, and in 1990, I left *ADS* and went to work for *Lavender & Wyatt*."

"So in summation, your accomplishments at *CDS* were? I need you to be specific," I stated.

He answered, "Around 1991 through '92, I created my own way of program design in RPG using my knowledge of PL/1, COBOL, Basic, and RPG by-passing the cycle, as well as created my own role screens. In addition, I was also one of the first to electronically transmit to *Blue Cross and Blue Shield*."

"And what exactly is RPG?" I asked for clarification.

"It's a high-level programming language, which stands for Report Generator commonly used in business applications. It's an IBM proprietary programming language."

"So you were working through IBM?" I asked.

"Actually, I was working on the client's *IBM* Computer Systems but not directly with *IBM*.

However, at the time I checked with *IBM* and all over the US and could find no one doing this," he clarified, "So after checking around I decided that writing X-MODEM in on the AS400 would allow us to communicate directly to PC's."

"And you got nothing by way of credit for your having redesigned RPG's functionality?" I asked, tugging at the thread just a little more as I sought consistency in his replies.

"No," but life got more interesting.

"Hmm," was all I said as I continued jotting down my notes.

*

OFF THE RECORD … In April of 1987, 28 years ago, IBM and Microsoft released OS/2, a historical new development that revolutionized operating systems. Later exclusively used by IBM, the name stands for "Operating System/2". OS/2 was intended as a protected mode successor of PC DOS, which made it possible to create "Family

Mode" applications; text mode applications
capable of working both systems.

In 1987 – though overall revenues were still
down - thereby continuing a 2-year trend - IBM's
gross income was $54.2 billion, a 5.8% increase
over 1986.

IBM Highlights 1985 – 1989 PDF. (n.d.).

3 THE BEGINNING

"I was employed at *Lavender & Wyatt* Systems, Inc. out of Little Rock from 1990 until May of 1992. By then I already had about eight years of programming experience under my belt when I decided to take things to the next level by creating communications between PC's and IBM computers, thus eliminating the need for PC Support. My online automatic posting program for medical electronic claims in addition to medical billing processing rapidly expanded from 3-5 different states, and the search/roll screen processing and program process I created ultimately made AS400 more PC-like and dummy proof for users," Stuart continued, as he recited the next phase of his professional development.

"As a result, I asked Mickey Lavender about the possibility of starting a business to do medical claims transmissions with the clearing house and a protocol process allowing the IBM System AS400 to communicate directly with PC's," Stuart then paused as if back-tracking in order to retrieve additional pertinent information cataloged somewhere within the chambers of his mind.

Then he continued, "If you remember, I had already created a programming structure for RPG programming without using the RPG cycle. This design ended up being a conglomerate of all my knowledge of COBOL, Basic, PL/1, and RPG all combined into one," Stuart explained.

"As previously stated, at the time I thought it would be good to be able to interact direct from the AS400 to PC's. So I decided that writing X-MODEM in on the AS400 would allow us to communicate directly. It was then I asked Mickey if I should get credit for all my creations, and the next thing I know, Dick Wyatt's son – Rick – is telling me, 'If they fire you, I'm going to quit.'"

Even today, Stuart seemed surprised by the statement as if he should have guessed at that point something sinister might be going on behind the scenes, but his perceptions clouded his vision. Although at the time he had thought himself too valuable to let go, two weeks later, immediately upon his return following a sick day, he was handed a check in exchange for his key. Thus Mickey Lavender had fired him.

This time it's my turn to pause for reflection. I shake my head in obvious disbelief, thinking to myself, "How can someone who had obviously proven his value instantly become a liability in need of dismissal?"

Greed was my obvious assumption – along with the necessity for opportunity. After all, it's difficult to pick a man's pocket when he's looking straight at you. With Stuart out of the picture, it was easy to take credit for his designs and then peddle them off systematically in exchange for money and favors.

"So am I right? Did they fuck you over?" I asked humbly, needing the confirmation but dreading it at the same time.

"Let me put it this way, Lavender & Wyatt – along with John Fuller – arranged for the sale of my software developments and then fired me. As a result, two weeks later, Rick Wyatt quit working for his dad and called to ask if I want to go into business with him, and foolishly I told him, 'No,' because I was going into business with my old friend, Paul Lancaster."

"So for the record …" Stuart paused and checked to make certain the recorder was on as I persisted with my prompting, "Let's recap your accomplishments at *Lavender & Wyatt* before moving on to your next venture."

"Okay … I used my knowledge of COBOL, Basic, PL/1 and RPG to create a new RPG design language, which I used to create a new system for medical health billing, including auto-postings. In addition I came up with the idea for electronic transfers between a PC and IBM AS400 and finally I made the mistake of asking Mickey Lavender and Dick Wyatt for a percentage of what I had created, and that got me canned."

"Amazing – but not in a good way," I responded.

*

OFF THE RECORD … Following is an excerpt copied and pasted directly from LWSI's homepage, which serves to define the company's corporate image:

Grounded in industry-standard accounting practices, LWSI's essentially provides the foundation and depth of functionality critical to improving overall financial performance through improved operational efficiencies like:

- Single data entry points
- Limiting services performed to those specifically authorized for the client and provider

- *Linking all services generated by agency personnel to a general ledger that serves as the backbone of the system*

Now, 36 years later, and with satisfied clients across the country, LWSI is positioned as one of the leading provider of information management solutions for behavioral healthcare providers.

Lwsi.com. (n.d.).

*

This cannot help but beg the question, "Could any of this have been possible without the contributions of one former employee whose creative genius revolutionized the way medical billing and accounting was being performed over twenty-four years ago?"

Maybe, but then again it might have been a long time in coming – if ever – and as a result, LWSI might never have become the driving force within the medical accounting industry that they are today. In addition, I have to wonder, back in 1991 where was the accountability when it came to the more intangible qualities found in ethics, good business practices and generally doing the right thing?

There should be a moral code of conduct constantly at play between any company and its employees that protects a worker's intellectual property whether it's clearly stated in its employee handbook or not, but perhaps I'm a little too idealistic and naïve. After all, we are a capitalist nation whose only line of conduct that's ever truly revered – much less respected - is the bottom line when it comes to profits and losses, but I can't help thinking it's a sad statement of our current affairs when the lessons we learn as adults have to come at such a high price.

*

EXHIBIT A. Following is an excerpt from Stuart's notes written during that time as it directly related to his creation of a new programming language:

I designed my programs by combining my knowledge of PL/1, Cobol, Basic & RPG. and I did away with IBM's RPG cycle. 1991, 1992.

I then decided that it would be good to be able to interact direct from the AS400 to PC's via ASYNC LINE. I checked with IBM and all over the US and could find no-one doing this.

So after checking around I decided that writing XMODEM in on the AS400 would allow my us to communicate directly to PC's.

4 FRIENDS IN LOW PLACES

"So you've stated during the end of your tenure with LWSI, old friends started coming around. Who were they exactly?" I asked in an effort to transition to the next position on his resume'.

"Paul Lancaster, Doug Danvers and Larry Edwards," he answered matter-of-factly, knowing full well I knew Paul and Doug the same way I'd gotten to know him … by growing up together while attending the same school.

"Who's Larry Edwards?" I asked, being unfamiliar with the name.

"He's an industrial sales rep and Paul's 'Big Brother' from his fraternity back at OBU

(Ouachita Baptist University).

*

"Funny story … he used to play basketball for Bryant back in high school. One time when they were playing Lakeside, Paul, Doug and I figured out you could wrap a piece of tape around a bobby pin forming a cone and then blow it like a dart, and it'd travel about fifty feet. We got Larry in the leg during a game, and he got pissed off. He probably got a technical, because he went up and down the court giving our stands a double bird. We instantly tossed the evidence up under the stands. He never knew who did it until college, and he was still hot about it."

Stuart and I both shared a good laugh. Old times were good times before life got too complicated, and friends were people you could actually count on back then.

*

It cannot help but feel unnerving – perhaps even a little nauseating – once you discover someone you once believed trustworthy is not. If

I felt an almost instant sense of betrayal upon the mere mention of some of Stuart's closest friend's names, I couldn't possibly imagine what Stuart must have felt the moment he realized those same childhood friends he once believed he could entrust with his life had turned up from low places.

The irrationality of it all must have torn away at every fiber of his being - at least for a while - but as it often has a habit of doing, survival mode kicked in just in time to rescue him from some misplaced sentiment, and as a result, he stands as living testament to the need to *Keep your friends close and your enemies closer*, a quote once made famous by veteran actor, Marlon Brando, who portrayed Don Corleone in the original movie, *The Godfather*.

*

"I wanted to kill him," Stuart commented, instantly calling me back from my mental meanderings.

"Who did you want to kill, Paul?" I asked

somewhat startled.

"Yeah Paul," he answered as if I should know, but I didn't, at least not at first.

"You see, after leaving *Lavender & Wyatt*, I immediately went into business with Paul thus becoming a partner in *Engineered Instruments*. So when Rick Wyatt quits working for his dad and Mickey and then calls to ask if I'd like to start a business together, I was already paired up with Paul. From the onset everything looked great. After all, what could be better than going into business with an old high school friend?"

"At what point did everything go south?" I asked.

"As time went by, I recognized Paul was not dependable. He developed a drug habit and he didn't want to work. Eventually I gave in – to some degree – because you can't co-exist in chaos unless you become a part of it. Next Paul and his wife get separated, and he starts taking money without telling me anything about it," Stuart confided.

*

I couldn't help thinking about that old adage everyone has heard at one time or another, *never loan money or go into business with a friend* …. Why is it people continue to try and beat those odds time and time again only to have the hypothesis proven correct one more time? It seemed as if *Engineered Instruments* was just another one of the many casualties that could be offered up as 'Exhibit A' when friendship goes on trial.

*

"I tried to stick it out and get Paul to work, but instead we ended up signing an agreement in which he was to pay me the $27,000 he owed me," Stuart continued, "and then the next thing we know Paul and I get dropped from *Air Monitor*.

"Instantly, we go to Sam Strange - an attorney with the well renowned Bloom Law Firm - and another attorney named Mike Heart who represented both our interests against *Air*

Monitor. Then once again Paul rips me off, and this time we end up going our separate ways. Although he signs another agreement to pay me, he doesn't."

"I have to have more details. Without them, it's impossible to paint a clear picture of just what happened," I confess.

"I'm afraid the details are sketchy at best," Stuart replied, "because even I have tried without success to get to the heart of exactly what happened. However - looking back - the case supposedly concluded in *non-prejudice*, but neither Paul nor his lawyers will tell me the results. In addition, Mike Heart told me I'd have to pay him for the time it took to uncover the ruling, but in the end, he didn't divulge whatever it was he uncovered."

Then Stuart goes on to say, "So next I call Sam Strange - who had since left his lucrative position with the Bloom Law Firm - in order to attend ministry school. He divulges that there had been between $500,000 and $750,000 there, but he stops short of revealing anything more in the way of details," Stuart pauses.

"I have to wonder, why Sam Strange ended up going to divinity school. Was it because he had a sudden calling? Or more likely because he needed to distance himself from continued exposure to the total lack of ethics he'd experienced in this case? Only he knows for certain, and he didn't disclose his reasons to me."

"Well in that case couldn't you go back to Mike Heart and pressure him for greater discovery?" I asked.

"That's a logical assumption, but it's always been my opinion that Mike Heart got my part of the settlement. Otherwise why would he continue representing Paul against me when Paul supposedly had no money? Either that or they had some kind of side agreement," he stated, in answer to my question.

"In addition, another friend of fifteen years tells me in confidence that *Air Monitor's* lawyers told him there was money there, and I should call them, but when I did they wouldn't speak to me."

"So you kept running into road blocks no matter which direction you turned?" I asked in an effort to confirm he'd tried everything.

"Even today I still cannot unearth the results of our lawsuit against *Air Monitor*. It's as if they've been buried in some unmarked grave in a dense field in the middle of nowhere. It's like looking for the proverbial needle in a hay stack only to decide after months of digging, *it just isn't there.*

"Subsequently, I also found out the programs I'd created while in partnership with Paul had been sold. However, I never received credit or payment," Stuart concluded.

*

OFF THE RECORD ... A fact worth noting, when Stuart split with Paul, he took all of the software he'd created for Engineered Instruments and stored it in his dad's garage. This fact will eventually become a key factor as future chapters unfold.

*

The dissolution of the partnership and the subsequent lawsuit during 1994 permanently disbanded Engineered Instruments, which devastated Stuart personally and created problems with his wife at that time. As a result, he began deer hunting a lot in order to take his mind off his problems and to try and relieve some of the stress he was under, but it seems a creative mind never really takes a day off when another old friend – Doug Danvers – repays a $30 debt to Stuart with a pair of deer antlers, explaining their value with regard to the hunt.

Then during autumn of 1995, a cousin of Stuart's, named Allen, told him about a huge buck that ended up giving Stuart 'buck fever' once they meet face-to-face, "He was a foot taller than all the other deer with a rack to match his size," Stuart recalled. His subsequent missed opportunity was detailed in a letter he'd written to Browning Arms.

In his quest to bag this particular deer, Stuart learned deer are hardly ever fooled more than once. So in order to replicate the sound of a deer's antlers rattling, he invented 'Rattle-Buck'.

5 RATTLE-BUCK

"Tell me about *Rattle*-Buck. How did it work exactly?" I asked.

"It was a remote control antler rattling device, a self-monitoring, recharging system that worked independently without interruption. It monitored scent, motion and sound. It was also a multi-button, digital transmission system with solar charging capabilities.

"I was hoping this invention would make good for all the problems I'd put my family through, but at the time, little did I know it was just the beginning of more," Stuart confided with a noticeable tone of regret in his voice.

*

It instantly became apparent my introduction to *Rattle-Buck* had inadvertently opened up old wounds that had refused to heal, even with the passage of time. I wished in that moment I had some magic wand, some words of wisdom capable of making him believe it wasn't his entire fault, but alas I felt inadequate to do so. All I could really do was try and tell his side of the story and how it had affected him over the years.

Throughout our numerous discussions, I had become increasingly aware Stuart blamed himself for the collapse of his marriage and all he'd put his family through, while I – with an outsider's perspective – saw it differently. He couldn't help reacting the way any of us might under similar circumstances. It's difficult - albeit impossible - to behave sane in insane situations.

Thus I began to see my contributions in this matter as something more than just being a storyteller. I was providing a means to give him peace the same way I had once found it for myself, by putting my story out there in hopes others may come to understand the choices we make as individuals have a sort of *ripple effect* in terms of how they affect the people around us. Once this lesson is taken to heart, it becomes far more difficult to assert one's preferences for the sake of self alone considering you know others might be hurt in the process.

*

While searching through old photos, he continued telling me about his prized invention, "Initially, there was a lot of excitement surrounding *Rattle-Buck*. I even met with then Arkansas Governor, Mike Huckabee, by way of the Invention Symposium held each year in Little Rock, which in turn ended up garnering a nice interview leading to a spread in the *Arkansas Democrat-Gazette*. I was even going to introduce it at the *Shot Show* but I didn't have a prototype yet, and my booth was cancelled so I missed the show. However, I did make it to the *Big Buck Classic*."

*

"Your notes say something about Dallas Semiconductor. How did they fit into the equation?" I inquired.

"*Dallas Semiconductor* related to electronics. At that time, there were no boards made up to do things like regulate diodes. Simply put, a diode is a semiconductor device with two terminals which allow the flow of current in one direction. This was the kind of technology necessary to make *Rattle*-Buck work effectively while transmitting to a remote location.

"I had a list of companies I'd gotten from out of the library who were developing the kind of technology I needed as it related to transistors," Stuart further explained, "By the way, did you know the first transistor was invented by a guy named William Shockley?"

"No!" I said, "Any relation?" I asked intrigued, "Maybe you came by your talents naturally."

Stuart shrugged his shoulders before continuing, "I also contacted *Overhead Door* and

Motorola. Basically, I was talking to anyone and everyone who had developed the pertinent technology I needed to refine my invention. In legal terms, I guess you could say I was doing my due diligence.

"I then went on to hire Ray Docks, a patent attorney who worked for B*right, Maser and Tokens* down on Main Street in Little Rock, to file my first patent, and he sent my patent to a draftsman named Dennis Little down in Florida. A couple days later, Ray told me Dennis worked for a company that promoted products and this got me thinking …" his voice trailed off.

"Thinking about what exactly?" I asked puzzled.

"It opened up a can of worms I suppose – some possibly good, others bad. To expand on that, I had to ask myself, 'Was Ray shopping my invention around for his benefit or mine?' After all, he had sent my confidential information to someone unbeknownst to me and without my permission. However – on the other hand – was he

46

just exhibiting enthusiasm because he saw a wealth of potential, in which case would've been good for me?"

I shook my head thinking out loud, "I don't know. It's impossible to crawl inside someone else's mind and know what they're thinking much less what motivated their behavior. But in terms of my own personal experience, while I may have originally hired an attorney to represent my personal interest, in the end it at least seemed Ray Docks had been working to further his own agenda all along."

"Exactly!" Stuart exclaimed in concurrence.

"Anyway, a few days later Ray told me Dennis may not be finished in time for the *Buck Arama* show on January 24th and that he needed to send it over to a man in Dallas, which is why I asked him to sign an agreement not to send the prototype all over the country, but he refused to sign, and the patent was filed on time," Stuart confided.

"Then that should tell you everything you

needed to know in terms of whose interest he was actually working to serve," I said, stating my somewhat jaded opinion, which had unfortunately been colored by my own past experience.

*

"In preparation for *Buck Arama*, I learned of a local man named Ted Drysdale from Vilonia, Arkansas who had represented *Remington Arms* for seventeen years. He agreed in advance to see me at the show.

"By the time the show actually came, my booth was ready, and I was so swamped with people, I couldn't even take a break to go to the facilities. When Ted arrived he immediately introduced himself, took one look at Rattle-Buck, and it was as if his mind shot off to another world, and suddenly he couldn't hear me or speak back coherently. All he could do was mutter out loud, *this will be huge volume*. Needless to say my wife, Diana, and I were excited. Finally, this was going to be the thing that launched my career and secured my family," Stuart said, with a degree of the excitement that had once been still noticeably audible even today.

*

"Not long after the show, Ted signed a protection agreement and took my invention to one of his manufacturers. Then after a few weeks it was returned with the message they couldn't assemble it, implying they had not used it. However, both aerosol cans were emptied, which strongly suggested otherwise," he stated categorically as if to confirm his own suspicions.

"Then Ted tells me *Wisconsin Pharmacal* is interested, but they will not sign my non-disclosure agreement, and I will not sign theirs, which basically equated to my first and second experience with false hope," Stuart continued.

"So next I spoke to Diana's uncle, Jim Moore, who then took me to *Ben Pearson Archery* in Oklahoma. He asked me to give them a brochure and to go speak with them, which I did. I later heard they were bought out by *Coleman Lantern*."

*

"Time goes by while I continue to seek a manufacturer. So next I spoke with Mickey Yu, my patent examiner, who suggested I file a CIP to better cover my patent."

According to USLEGAL.COM, Carriage and Insurance Paid is a legal term used in international contracts. A seller first assumes all risks and expense for delivering a product to the buyer. The risks then transfer from the seller to the buyer at the point where goods are delivered to the first carrier.

"Mickey Yu strongly suggested Ray Docks was not representing my best interests," Stuart said, while I continued to jot down notes in my own perfected shorthand.

"By July of 1995, I informed Ray of my newest modifications and suggested we add them with a CIP. He said okay and then told me I needed to send them to Dennis in Florida, because he, himself, was going to be in Florida vacationing," Stuart disclosed as if just now realizing his mistake these many years later.

"But that's not all," he went on to say, "I drew up a letter granting Ray my Power-of-Attorney and filed it with the patent office."

"Stuart, you were way too trusting," I couldn't help interjecting my thoughts. Part of me felt so badly for how he'd been used and taken advantage of, but another part of me couldn't help wondering how he didn't know better. After all the secrets we have are only as good as those we're willing to keep. Whether speaking in terms of some unique spin on words or a newly developed invention, it can only truly be protected as long as it remains in the creator's hands.

I understood the burdens of trying to market something in order to be successful, but I also understood the necessity that a certain amount of secrecy be constantly woven within the process. For instance, in the South it's a time-honored tradition for most good cooks to withhold one or two ingredients when passing on an *old family recipe*. She may be flattered that she was asked, but she'd never dream of another's interpretation being as good as her own. As such, I've asked for very few recipes over the years, preferring instead to stick with what I know.

Stuart continued, "I know, you're right. I was young, and hindsight is always 20/20."

"I'm sorry. I don't mean to pour salt on a still open wound. You were young and you were a good man. You expected the people you were working with to be as forthright and honorable as yourself," I paused, "Partially - maybe even mostly - it's not your fault, but unfortunately some lessons we're forced to learn the hard way."

*

"Anyhow, by October of 1995, I made contact with a company out of Springdale, Arkansas named *Artech*. They invited me in to demo *Rattle-Buck* and to discuss the possibilities. The first thing I noticed when I walked into their lobby was my name on the Welcome Board, and that made me feel good.

"Consequently I met with Steve Ballard -

their Vice President - a marketing person named Rhonda and an engineer. After demoing the product, I discussed my plans for its future design. I also told them how to get more power from a battery than the actual voltage of the battery in order to keep it from burning up, and they decided to sign a non-disclosure," Stuart continued, "I left with the understanding they would call me in two days to send me schematics as well as the fact they intended to discuss packaging at our next meeting. They also agreed to produce two prototypes for the upcoming *Shot Show* in January of '96.

"But from that point on nothing worked out with them," Stuart confessed, "Eventually Steven Ballard ended up telling me there weren't any schematics, while Rhonda confided she'd never seen a prototype, but confessed she had seen the schematics."

"So what you're saying is according to the information you were given, nothing was adding up," I stated in order to confirm his supposition.

*

"Moving forward, January is coming around so I called to confirm my booth space for the *Shot Show*, I ended up purchasing booth rental to the tune of $1100. However, by the time January rolled around, the prototype I was promised ended up being non-functioning, and I was forced to miss the show after all," and as a matter of consequence, I found out my booth had been mysteriously canceled, Stuart concluded.

"So, let me get this straight," I interrupted, "You were not the one to cancel your booth space? Did you ever find out who did?" I asked.

"The answer to both questions is no. I never canceled my reservation, and no, there was no way of tracking down who did," he said, which confirmed my suspicions.

"As a result, I hired another lawyer, and *Artech* returned the $500 I'd given them as down payment on the prototype, in addition to asking if I would sign a letter releasing them from any further damages or obligations, but I did not sign it. Therefore, *Artech* has never released all the information on exactly what they did with my project, which happened to have been part of the non-disclosure agreement," he paused.

"However, by the end of January, the beginning of February, they tried to nail me down to one prototype, which appeared to me to be an effort on their part to get around the non-disclosure," he revealed.

"At least you got your money back. I suppose that's something," I said, though I was pretty much disgusted by each and every turn of events.

"Please continue," I said as I prompted Stuart for more details.

"Then in January of 1996, I filed a patent on my digital electronic transmitter and receiver, and *Artech* ended up dropping me as a client," Stuart concluded.

"One postscript worth mentioning - just

another tricky little piece of the puzzle – one might say, I spoke to Gary Speed who worked with the Bloom Law Firm. I showed him everything I've had and asked him to complete my patent, but shortly afterwards he goes into business for himself and moves to New Jersey."

"Really?" I asked in amazement, "So this is the second attorney – both from the Bloom Law Firm – who ended up permanently leaving his post to pursue other interests after having been linked to you as a client? Don't you think that odd?" I go on almost as if I'm thinking out loud yet again, "I mean the Bloom Law Firm is the most widely acclaimed law firm in the state. Do you know how coveted a position in their firm would be? Hillary Clinton was once a partner in that firm."

Even though I say this, it's not exactly a revelation. Way back then, as First Lady of Arkansas, she was automatically high profile. Everyone who kept up with the news knew of her association.

*

"Moving on," Stuart began again, quickly checking to make certain we're still recording, "Then I hired Steve Garver, who I was told was the only local patent attorney. He told me to *stick to computers and he'll handle the patent.* He immediately took off to Ohio and California, while explaining he had offices in both California and New Jersey."

"Interesting, I wonder why he even mentioned New Jersey," I couldn't help interjecting, "What did that have to do with your patent?"

"I don't know," Stuart confessed, "Maybe nothing. The only link I had to New Jersey was when Gary Speed decided to abandon my case and relocate there."

"Sorry, I didn't mean to interrupt. I'm just trying to get a full understanding of the events as they played out chronologically. Please continue, what happened with Steve Garver?" I asked in an attempt to resume the discussion where it had left off …

Stuart continued, "Garver told me I needed a patent attorney, because people at the patent office often misplace and lose things, and that a good attorney can assist in these matters.

"Interestingly enough, since confiding this fact, I have not received all of my mail. Some of it's been lost, and other letters that arrived have been previously opened, but Steve did help me file my final action on the first patent and went on to write a continuation for me with regard to changes that I'd made," Stuart disclosed.

"Then on a subsequent visit to Steve's office, I showed him my electronic patent and signed over my power of attorney regarding the first patent and CIP. Then suddenly he started back-peddling and got very nervous. He told me to give him everything, even my drawings."

"And this didn't strike you as strange?" I inquired.

"Not at first. I was going on the advice of

my attorney who I had hired to protect my interests, but then he – Garver – hired another attorney named Trent Keisling in addition to a draftsman. Up to that point, Steve had always been accessible, but after Trent came on board, everything went through him," Stuart confided.

"So Trent Keisling became a sort of firewall insinuated between you and Steve Garver?" I asked.

"Yeah, I guess you could say that," he concluded.

"Anyway, during the course of a private conversation regarding my electronic patent, Keisling made a rather ominous reference to the effect, 'You know, if you keep messing with this, you might end up dead,' which was not exactly what I'd been waiting to hear," the frustration almost vacated at once, leaving a healthy dose of paranoia in its place.

I remain in silence, utterly speechless from what I'd just heard.

Following a lengthy pause, Stuart

continued, "He also told me there was $1,000,000 somewhere ...". (Three years ago at a local establishment)* Note:(One year ago I meet and asked Steve what happened to my $1,000,000 dollars. He left immediately, avoiding my question.)

"In May of 1996, I was in the process of mailing changes to my electronic patent at the Conway, Arkansas post office when I couldn't help noticing I was being followed by a man toting a backpack. He instantly went over to the clerk I'd just handed over my paperwork to in order to have it mailed when it appeared as if the postman gave the stranger an envelope resembling my patent, which he then placed in his backpack."

"Did you stop him or say anything?" I asked.

"No, but I did get a name from off his jacket. It appeared he was employed by a plastics company there in Conway," he said.

"Interesting," I said as I continued writing notes.

"What's interesting is despite my relocation back to Hot Springs and numerous attempts to forward my mail, all correspondence relating to my patent still manages to go to Conway even to this day," Stuart confided.

"That is kind of remarkable," I added.

"Anyway, from May of '96 until August of that same year, the patent office couldn't find my electronic patent response, so I decided to tell Steve about this, while confessing I'm pretty certain I know exactly where it is. Then shortly afterwards the patent office miraculously found my response and then offered to send back my money.

"Subsequently, Steve Garver started up another corporation with Dennis B. Hasse named *Garver & Hasse*. As of today, Garver will no longer speak to me directly preferring instead I send him everything in writing, although he did offer to drop all the monies I owed him.

"Following the break-up between Paul and myself, I was devastated. I didn't go back to work immediately. Eventually, Steve said he had someone interested in hiring me in Southern Arkansas, and together he and my dad sent me to work for *Chemx.*"

⋆

OFF THE RECORD ... A brief review of events reads as follows:

1. *While at Arkansas Data Services, Stuart is denied a raise during the course of his annual review, despite having directly contributed to the company's record revenues for that same year. Therefore, he left CDS to pursue a position with Lavender & Wyatt.*

2. *Stuart invented a program while working at Lavender & Wyatt designed to do automatic posting and billing for medical records, complete with roll screen technology without utilizing the RPG cycle. It was a brand new programming language for*

its time, performing certain tasks as directed.

3. *It was then Stuart asked his employers if he should receive credit for his creation.*

4. *During this same time, Stuart was approached by Rick Wyatt – one of the partner's sons – who confided, "If they fire you, I'm quitting."*

5. *Two weeks later, after returning from a sick day, Stuart is given his final check in exchange for his key.*

6. *By the time Rick Wyatt reached Stuart to ask if he'd like to start a business with him, he has already gone into what proves to be an ill-fated venture with his old friend, Paul Lancaster.*

7. *With their company now defunct, Stuart and Paul entered into a lawsuit.*

8. *From the beginning, the lawsuit against Paul Lancaster was dictated by unethical practices. Stuart's first lawyer – a man by the name of Donald R. Roberts - died and the second had a heart attack, in addition the judge's ruling has never been revealed to the plaintiff. During this time, Stuart's employer mysteriously sent him out of town each time a court date was scheduled. A fellow employee told Stuart he is under the 'witness protection program'.*

9. *Despite having stored his programs from his joint venture with Paul Lancaster in his dad's garage following the dissolution of their company, Stuart's programs are sold out from under him.*

10.   *Now seriously depressed, Stuart develops a hunting addiction to take his mind off his troubles.*

11.   *As a result, Stuart invented Rattle-Buck.*

12.   *Eventually, Artech fails to make good on their commitments, and Stuart misses the product's anticipated launch at the January 1996 Shot Show.*

13.   *Subsequently, everyone else he speaks to about his invention quickly drops him.*

14.   *Frustrated with his inability to develop Rattle-buck as he'd hoped, and after running into one brick wall after another, Stuart opts to take the position he's been offered in Eldorado, Arkansas.*

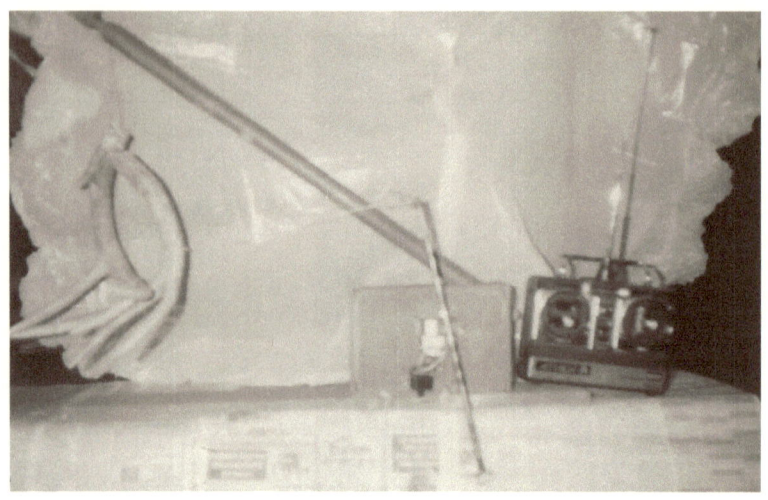

Figure 1. Represents the very first incarnation of *Rattle-Buck*, which was conceived from a pair of antlers intended to settle a debt between friends. It was then combined with spare parts found around the household to create a functioning device capable of detecting wildlife by picking up on their scent, motion and sound while sending those images to a remote location.

Figures 2. & 3. (On the following page) show the progression of the device as it was moved to a test location somewhere in the in the woods. At this point, it is a self-monitoring, re-charging system with solar capabilities.

Figure 4. Shows how the device could be mounted as opposed to resting on a tripod.

Figure 5. On Page 70 shows the device is fully operational with aerosol spray.

Figure 6. On Page 71 shows the initial sales brochure; Note the ^{TM} symbol by the Rattle-Buck name denoting the Trademark.

Figures 7, 8. And 9. On Pages 72 & 73 show Stuart's original schematics during the developmental phase.

Figures 10. & 11. On Pages 74 & 75 Shows the *Arkansas Democrat-Gazette* article, which featured Stuart's Rattle-Buck Invention during the *Arkansas Inventors Symposium* and subsequently ran in the newspaper's *Style* Section on July 11, 1995.

Figure 12. On Page 76 Shows the Trademark Awarded to Stuart for his Rattle-Buck invention, which is dated on January 28, 1995 and signed by the then Arkansas Secretary of State, Sharon Priest.

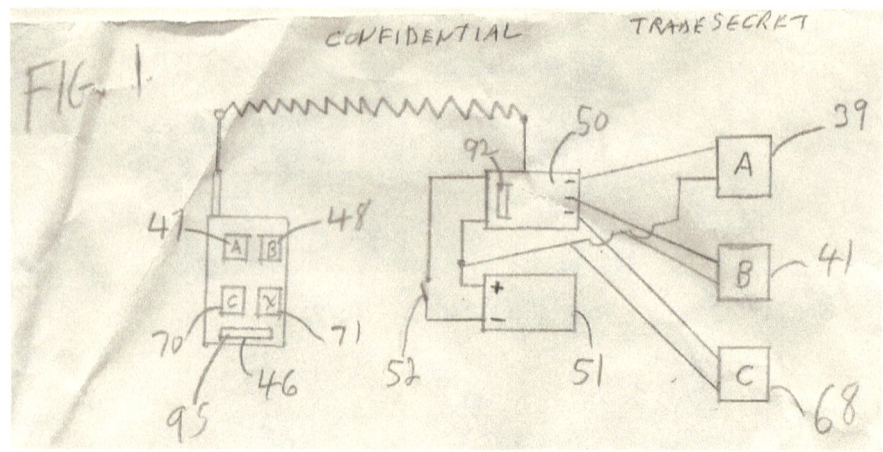

Figure 7.

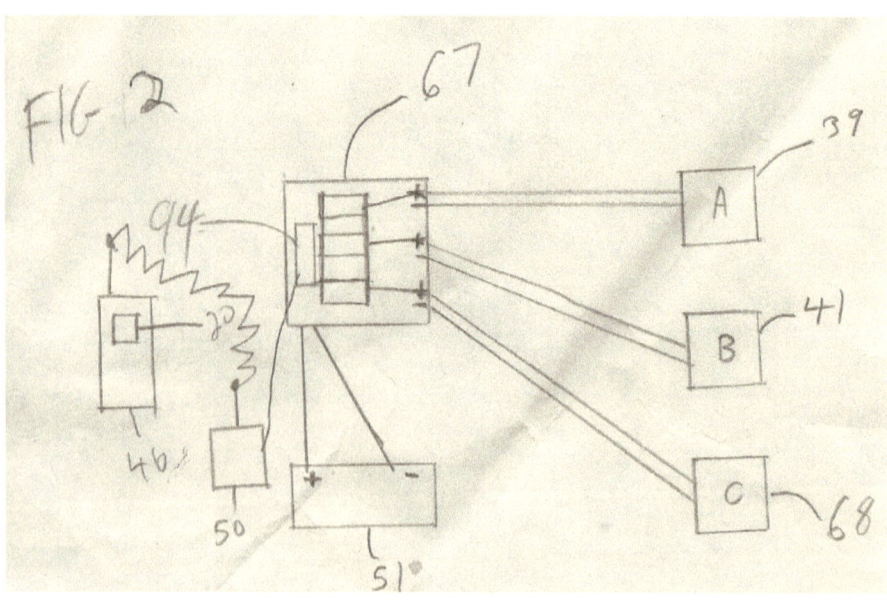

Figure 8.

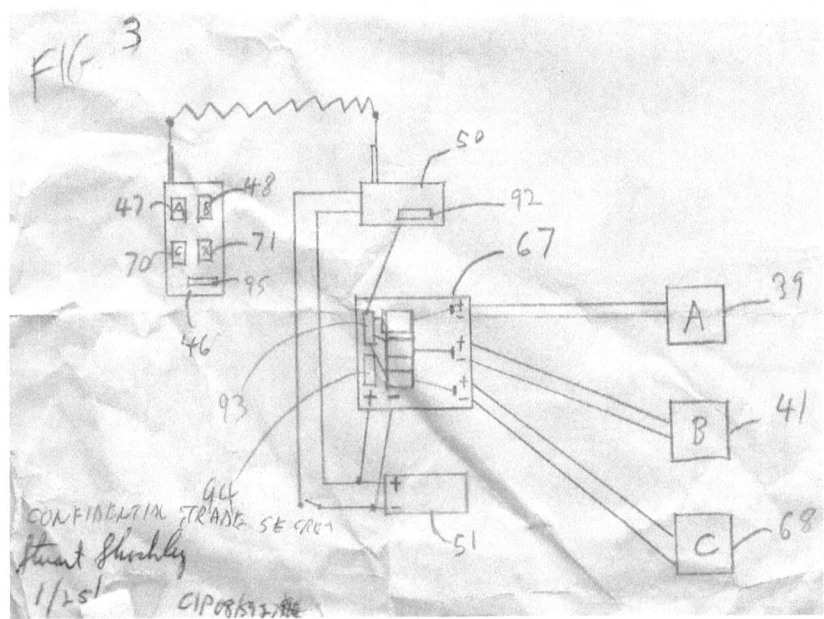

Figure 9.

BUILDING A
TTER MOUSETRAP

Photos/MORRIS RICHARDSON II

s Minnow Water Circulating System.

INVENTOR Bobbie Little Young (right) and Barbara Spradley came up with UltraMax, a portable rinsing cap and shampoo bowl for use in beauty salons, nursing homes and hospitals.

Creators display their contrivances in hopes of striking it rich at Arkansas Inventors Symposium.

BY TONY MOSER/ SPECIAL TO THE DEMOCRAT-GAZETTE

Ah, the great pantheon of American inventors: Eli Whitney and the cotton gin, Thomas Alva Edison and the electric lamp, Alexander Graham Bell and the telephone, Stuart Shockley and the Rattle Buck.

Wait a minute ... Who's Stuart Shockley? And what's a Rattle Buck?

Well, Shockley — a computer consultant and programmer from Maumelle — is one of the 60 Arkansas inventors who turned out to display their wares at the recent Arkansas Inventors Symposium at the Hall of Industry on the Arkansas State Fairgrounds. And the Rattle Buck is ... well, you'd almost have to see it to believe it.

What Shockley has devised is a radio-controlled deer lure. The deer hunter sits in his deer stand and commands the Rattle Buck with the toggle switches on a transmitter. The tripod-mounted lure has deer horns that rattle against one another as an auditory enticement (thus the name), and an aerosol sprayer that shoots doe or buck urine into the air to tingle the olfactory senses.

Nearby deer hear the noise, catch the scent and scamper toward the lure to find out what's going on. When they come into range, the hunter blows 'em away.

"A deer doesn't like it when another deer horns in on his territory," Shockley explains. "So, when they hear the rattle and catch the scent, they'll come around to check it out."

He adds that a new, improved version of the Rattle Buck will also feature a mechanized deer call, which will issue imitation "bleats," thus adding another auditory weapon to the device's high-tech quiver.

What would move a person to invent such a device? Well, it seems there was a Moby Dick — or, as the case may be, Moby

See INVENTORS, Page 8E

8E • TUESDAY, JULY 11, 1995 • •

Inventors

• Continued from Page 1E

Deer — in Shockley's past. For the inside story, it's necessary to turn to his wife, Diana, a Maumelle teacher.

"He had been trying for two years to get this great granddaddy buck deer, but he hadn't had much luck," Diana explains. This led her camouflage-wearing Captain Ahab to construct his first Rattle Buck prototype, and she ventured into the forest with him to harpoon the great beast.

"When those horns rattled, you could just hear the deer suddenly coming," Diana Shockley says, marveling at her husband's handiwork. But, as was the case with Ahab, things didn't quite work out as planned for Stuart Shockley.

The great granddaddy took the bait of the Rattle Buck, and appeared beneath the deer stand: "My husband was hunting with a crossbow, and he shot the buck, but it didn't die right then. It ran off, and we never found it."

The stuff of great American myth, to be sure. But, that Melvillian outcome aside, Shockley is enjoying great success hunting with the Rattle Buck. And he's waiting on patent approval from the U.S. Patent Office, while also looking for investors, manufacturers and marketers to raise his creation toward the next level of entrepreneurial stardom.

Photos/MORRIS RICHARDSON II

STUART SHOCKLEY, inventor of Rattle Buck.

Figure 11.

75

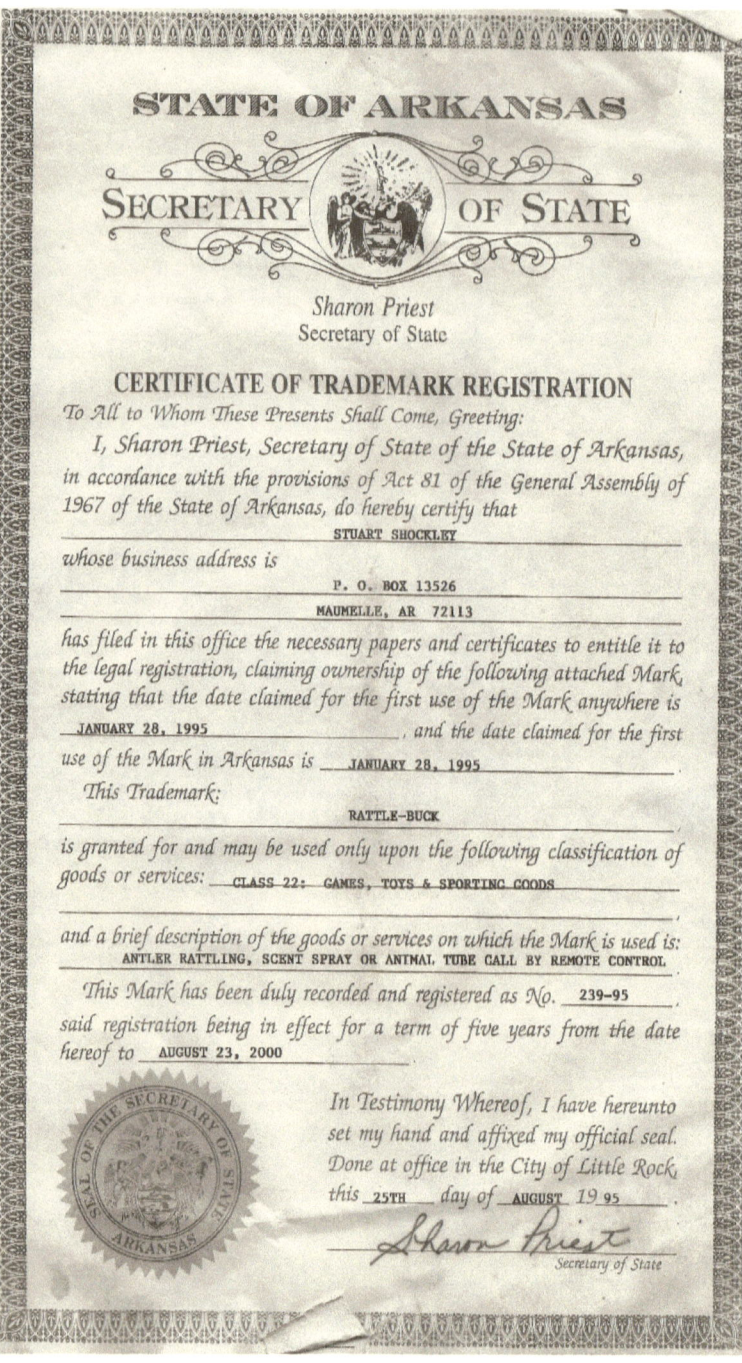

Figure 12.

6 WHAT HAPPENS IN ELDORADO

"I'm sitting on the couch one day when I get a phone call from Ann Mulready of Snelling & Snelling," Stuart began.

"And who is she," I asked.

"An employment agent," he answered, "She'd been given my name by Bill Heron, a gentleman who lived in the same building as my dad in Maumelle (Arkansas), who eventually moved down to Florida.

After not working for so long, I'm excited, so I go down for the interview and get the job."

"In Eldorado?" I asked for verification.

"Yes, Eldorado," Stuart confirmed, "Ann tells me to go to Eldorado and work for *Chemx* for two years as a programmer/analyst and then come back and sue whoever is messing with my invention for 40 million.

"*Chemx* asked me to sign a non-disclosure agreement," he confided.

"Really? Why? What does *Chemx* do?" I ask in rapid fire succession without hesitating to get an answer between questions.

"*Chemx* is an incineration facility that is fully permitted to incinerate a variety of hazardous, non-regulated and *special handling* wastes," he replied, while looking online and reading directly from envirosource.com, "It goes on to say *waste types that can be accepted include: wastewaters, inorganics, organics, paint sludges, pesticides, reactives, halogenated and halogenated solvents, TCLP toxic metals, acids, caustics, and oils.*"

"That's a pretty ominous sounding list," I couldn't help commenting. All these chemicals … I couldn't help thinking to myself. What had we done to the environment in the name of progress?

"Agreed, which was why I'm not comfortable

with signing the non-disclosure agreement. I even asked around to other employees as to whether or not they were asked to sign any such agreement and I was told *no*.

"Then I spoke with both my dad and Steve Garver and each told me to sign the non-disclosure, and then *Chemx* leaned on me to the effect that if I refused to sign, I may not be working there, so I added my own addendum, and then *they* refused to sign. As a result, I ended up working there anyway." He concluded.

*

"As time goes by, chemical smells in my office began to make me feel weak and dizzy," Stuart revealed while on one wavelength and then quickly reverted to another making it difficult to digest at first.

"In the meantime, they took my programs that I had saved on tape to their downtown office with the supposed intent to download them to their computer so that I can continue to use my samples for programming. Upon returning, they told me they could not put it on their system."

"Was that unusual?" I asked.

In answer Stuart said, "It happens when one operating system doesn't speak the same language as another. So technically it's possible."

*

And then he reverted back to his original thought, as if unable to quite let it go, "After a month or so, of having worked there, a very distinct combination of a sweet, perfume like smell followed by a harsh odor, continued to contaminate my surroundings. It was even in my apartment for three days! It was so strong, I choked and had difficulty breathing, and then I became faint and light-headed. I slept by an open window for three consecutive nights before moving out of the place."

"Was there anything else that prompted your move," I asked.

"Absolutely, once I discovered that a vent ran from my apartment directly across the hall to another apartment. A man from *Great Lakes*

Chemical stayed there. Of course there was no way of knowing for certain, but I couldn't help wondering if that smell had somehow originated from his apartment," Stuart asserted, as if he needed nothing more in the way of suspicion to back up his decision to move. In terms of evidence, it's nothing more than circumstantial, but the coincidence between the distinctive odors was uncanny and seemed a bit far-fetched to reason it as mere coincidence.

Then, he went on to say, "Around that same time, I began to notice I was being followed on numerous occasions. Each Friday night, I was followed from Eldorado to Hampton on my way home."

"Is there any way of knowing who was behind that?" I asked.

"That would only be supposition on my part," Stuart confided, "By this time, and without even trying, I'd managed to ruffle some pretty important feathers. Going down that list, it could have been any one of them I suppose," he said in conclusion.

*

"One day, I was asked to go through a health and safety class at *Chemx*, so as a result, I'm taken on a plant tour. I was guided through the warehouse where the barrels are received, and I couldn't help noticing all the warehouse personnel were wearing respirators, but those of us taking the tour were not offered any such protective device. We traveled down the aisles, through the barrels toward the back where we stopped to hear a talk about something.

"It was there I smelled it, that same sweet smell I'd been inhaling in my workspace and apartment. I instantly became very weak, nauseous and light-headed," Stuart explained as if it had just happened yesterday.

"Did anyone else appear to notice your reaction?" I asked.

"If they did, it wasn't apparent, and I tried as best I could to keep my thoughts and feelings to myself rather than appear visibly shaken," he confided.

Then continuing with his story, Stuart's voice took on the sound of a cool monotone, "We then moved to the back of the incinerator area where once again they paused for another brief discussion, and I could see other workers about fifty feet upwind from where we stood all clad in self-contained, sealed bodysuits complete with head gear, while presumably working on hazardous materials. There I noticed a different smell than before and once again I became very weak.

"Despite the fact my feet felt like anchors, I kept moving around. I suppose anxiety took hold, and I was afraid I might fall down or pass out if I didn't keep moving," his voice now trailed off just a bit.

Mesmerized, I sat in silence as I waited to hear the outcome. I didn't wish to break his concentration or redirect his line of thought. I knew these were difficult memories, but the details were important in terms of getting his story right.

"I don't know how I did it …" Stuart began again, "finish the tour that it, but I remember clearly that once I left the plant, my symptoms and breathing slowly began to subside, and everything returned to normal."

*

"Then while programming in my office one day, I began to smell that same sweet smell. Straightaway my eyes began to water, my vision blurred, and I began to have difficulty breathing. I managed to get up and stagger out of my office to go and see if anyone else was experiencing these same symptoms only to discover that all five employees in my vicinity were gone," Stuart said with a note of astonishment still present in his voice.

"Afterwards, I spoke with my boss and other people in my department about this, and it was then one of the girls took me out the back door of the office and showed me a return air vent in the mechanic's supervisor's office," he said, instantly visualizing that moment.

"Here," she had said pointing, "that's where they could put the smell."

For Stuart that moment served as validation for all that he'd been going through since arriving on the scene. This one brave soul in the form of a young woman wasn't telling him he was crazy or that he'd only imagined what he thought had happened to him. Instead, she was showing him access, which at that time doubled as a plausible explanation as to how someone could systematically be poisoning him.

*

"Then on another day, I was sent to work with people down in the truck receiving area. I was asked to alter a program so that information on the barrels could be manually changed," Stuart said.

"What?" I asked, unable to contain my disbelief, "All of that hazardous waste is so heavily regulated – and for good reason – I might add. No one can just decide to change the labeling at will. Think how potentially dangerous that could be? Entire populations could wind up being contaminated."

"Everything you're saying is correct, but at the time I told them I would need to get permission from my supervisor, and I was told in return, *you don't need to do that*, and that was it," he concluded. "I refused to do as told."

*

OFF THE RECORD ... It would be easy enough to explain away Stuart's perceived reactions to chemical exposure during this time. One might suggest hyper-sensitivity to all the chemicals naturally present within such an environment, or that due to his existing paranoia as it related to all that he had previously experienced prior to his taking a position with Chemx, such reactions were more or less imagined; however, such rationalizations become difficult – albeit impossible – once other as yet unrevealed details become apparent.

For instance, due to his continued suspicions, Stuart decided to take unplanned vacation time off. During this time, he stayed there locally in Eldorado with another former high school friend named Doug Danvers, who often worked atypical hours in his field of radiology. Days turned into weeks wherein Stuart lead a laidback existence while taking his mind off his troubles spending countless hours competing against Doug as they watched "Jeopardy" together from the comfort of home.

Prior to this unintended break, he had not submitted the necessary paperwork to take time off, and he had not spoken to his direct supervisor in advance with the intention of expressing any particular or personal need to do so, much less call in on a daily basis to at least feign sickness or something out of sorts. He did nothing but disappear for a period of time consisting of a week.

Upon his return, he was not chastised, fired or let go for insubordinate behavior. Instead, he was given his check and treated as if nothing unusual or out of the ordinary had occurred. So he ended up taking another 2 weeks off – more or less the same scenario – and this time returned to a raise in salary.

In terms of best corporate practices or even your common, run-of-the-mill employee handbook, there is no logical explanation as to what happened, but rather facts that beg further explanation while adding to the mystery surrounding this time.

*

In terms of trying to paint a picture that makes sense, I think it's worth pondering a couple of the events that led up to Stuart having been offered this position in the first place. The first has to do with his father and namesake.

Remember when Stuart and Paul Lancaster's partnership was disbanded, Stuart stored all of his programs (all of his intellectual property) – which were anything and everything of value – that he took from Engineered Instruments. Somewhere during the course of the ensuing lawsuit, all of this material disappeared and was presumably sold, and when Stuart was racing from out of town to attend the settlement of that case, he subsequently discovered his father had beaten him there and stood in his stead.

Even though Sam Strange – the attorney who had once been with the Bloom Law Firm but then left to attend the seminary – had alluded to a considerable amount of money that was 'there' Stuart was unable to track its whereabouts down, much less ever get a formal ruling in the case.

Greed is a funny thing capable of turning the people we think we know into perfect strangers once it takes hold of their imagination. How many people have been misled, taken advantage of or even killed as a means to cover up another's uncontrollable urge to take what doesn't belong to them? There's no real way of ever knowing that statistic, but it's not far-fetched to believe a father could steal from his own son and then try and justify having done so in order to pacify his own conscience.

But then guilt can be just as powerful an

emotion as greed when it comes to a father's love
for his son, which is why I think Robert Shockley
Senior – with the assistance of Steve Garver –
sought to secure a position for Stuart at a
stable company like Chemx and why he told his son
at one point after Stuart had expressed his
dismay, "At least you've got a job."

Stuart's father had been intimately
involved in the war that raged following Stuart
and Paul's break-up, only to witness continued
issues for his son surrounding Rattle-Buck, which
lead to a 3-year hiatus from work.

Although Robert Shockley's support was
undoubtedly genuine at that point, one might
continue to question the motives of Steve Garver,
who had previously failed Stuart miserably when
it came to protecting his Rattle-Buck invention.
He had already moved on to Florida, and at that
point, Stuart was nothing more than an irritating
former client, and thus he refused to take his
calls.

So why would Steve Garver care about what

happened to Stuart? And why would he help secure him a position at Chemx – a chemical incinerator – miles away from his home and situated in Eldorado, Arkansas? I think it at least fair to suspect his motives may not have been as pure as those of the father.

*

And finally, while in Eldorado, Stuart learned a unique phrase called 'trick-fuck' from his friend, Doug Danvers. Its meaning is rather simple and straight to the point. Apparently, by the time one learns they've been tricked, they're already fucked.

*

Figure 13. Page 93 represents the Non-Disclosure Agreement Chemx presented to Stuart as a condition of his employment. It was never signed.

Figure 14. On Page 94 Represents the Non-Compete Agreement Chemx presented Stuart with as a condition of his employment, and it too was never signed.

Figures 15. & 16. On Pages 95, 96. & 97.
Represent pages 1 & 2 of the Addendum, as well as
an Appendix Stuart presented to Chemx as
condition for him signing both the Non-Disclosure
and Non-Compete agreements; however, Chemx
refused signature, thus none of the agreements
were ever signed by either party involved.

 **INCORPORATED**

NON-DISCLOSURE AND NON-USE AGREEMENT

Gentlemen:

The undersigned recognizes that your business of recycling and/or disposal or sale of organic or inorganic chemical waste and the by-products of such waste involves specialized and proprietary knowledge, information, methods, processes, techniques, skills and heretofore undiscovered and valuable aspects thereof which are or may be unique and peculiar to you. I recognize that you have advertised, solicited, rendered services, obtained customers and expended money in the development and cultivation of your business and the skills required in said business. I acknowledge that any disclosure of such methods, processes, skills, financial data or other confidential or proprietary information would substantially injure your business, impair your investments and good will, injure the business and mandest your representatives and jeopardize your relationship with your supplies and customers and that the consequences thereof would be irreparable. I understand that any proprietary or financial information revealed to me by you remains the exclusive property of you and your successors and assigns, unless expressly stated otherwise in writing. The consideration for this agreement shall be your disclosures to the undersigned hereunder as provided below.

The undersigned agrees not to use, publish, disclose, divulge, communicate or reveal to any person, corporation, or parent organization, or to any officer, employee or agent of the undersigned directly or indirectly without the written consent of you, your successors and assigns, information spec foot forward such proprietary and secret character received by the undersigned or any person acting on behalf of the undersigned from you during the course of dealings and negotiations with you, concerning any of your methods, processes, techniques, equipment, skills, know-how or financial information regarding recycling and/or disposal or sale of organic or inorganic chemical waste, or the names of any of your customers or prospective customers.

All employees of the undersigned to whom any such confidential and/or proprietary information is disclosed, and any person, corporation, partnership, association, contractor, sub-contractor, subsidiary or parent organization and any officers, employees or agents thereof, to whom the undersigned shall divulge such secret, confidential and/or proprietary information with your written permission, shall be required to execute in advance a copy of this non-disclosure, non-use agreement, and the undersigned will immediately furnish you with an original signed copy thereof.

This agreement of confidentiality and non-use is to remain in effect for ten (10) successive years from and after the date of execution of it by the undersigned at which time, unless sooner terminated, the undersigned will return to you all copies of any data, drawings, notes and papers relating to your confidential and/or proprietary information all in the possession of the undersigned or under the control of the undersigned. The undersigned agrees individually and on behalf of all persons, partnerships or corporations which the undersigned represents hereon to use our best efforts to regain such materials that we may have given to any outside, subsidiary or parent organization. The undersigned binds himself and all persons for whom the undersigned now or thereafter shall act to treat all confidential and/or proprietary information pertaining to processing or recycling and/or disposal or sale of organic or inorganic chemical waste received from you as secret.

This agreement is independent of any enforceable patent rights that you may have or hereafter acquire for your methods, techniques, equipment or know-how.

It shall be your responsibility following execution of this agreement to disclose and describe in writing and specifically label and identify all aspects, features, techniques, methods and devices of the art of your processing, recycling and disposal and/or sale of organic or inorganic chemical wastes which are to be classified as secret by you and the subjects of these covenants not to disclose. The undersigned understands and agrees that said itemization of protected information shall become thereupon a part of this agreement as though stated in full herein, and the same shall be dated, and signed by you and the undersigned as Appendix A hereto.

The undersigned further agrees that if the undersigned or any person acting for the undersigned and bound hereby shall develop from information disclosed in Appendix A, any usable, patentable or otherwise registrable improvement upon any art, design, method or technique which shall utilize as a material part thereof any such information disclosed in Appendix A, then the undersigned shall refrain from disclosing the same to others and shall immediately notify and fully inform _____ of all facts of the same, and no action with regard to the use or patent search, application for patent or other registry thereof shall be initiated by the undersigned, or any person acting on behalf of the undersigned, without prior written agreement by you which shall mutually determine the respective rights of the undersigned and _____ herein.

It is understood that during the term hereof _____ may successfully achieve and develop additional and improved methods, techniques, equipment and knowledge utilizing the information contained in Appendix A, or otherwise which may be usable and valuable to the undersigned and that it may be desirable to _____ to make disclosure thereof to the undersigned subject to the covenants of secrecy contained herein, in furtherance of other agreements which may be made hereafter between us. The undersigned agrees that in said event the undersigned will enter into a like agreement of non-disclosure which may be separate or by addendum hereto at the election of _____.

The undersigned will take all reasonable and necessary steps to protect the confidentiality of the information herein disclosed by Appendix A. In addition, the undersigned recognizes and agrees that your remedy at law for the breach hereof would be inadequate. Therefore the undersigned covenants that in the event of any breach of this agreement by the undersigned, its agent, officers or persons acting on its behalf, you shall be entitled to appropriate equitable relief (including, but not limited to, injunctive relief or specific performance) in the addition to money damages.

Any controversy or claim between us arising out of or relating to this agreement of non-disclosure or the breach by the undersigned thereof shall be submitted at once to arbitration before one (1) arbitrator to be designated by the American Arbitration Association for hearing in Little Rock, Arkansas, in accordance with the rules of the American Arbitration Association. In the event of an award to you, judgment upon the award rendered by the arbitrator, including equitable relief, may be sought by you and enforced in any court having jurisdiction thereof.

This agreement shall be construed under the laws of the State of Arkansas for all purposes. Either party may request that all arbitration proceedings be conducted in secret, and that all documents, testimony and records shall be so heard and maintained in secret by the arbitrator, to be inspected only by the parties and their respective counsel who shall themselves agree in advance to treat all such information as confidential.

In the event that any provisions herein shall be held to be voidable or unenforceable by arbitration award or court decree, all other provisions herein shall remain in full force and effect.

All terms, conditions and covenants herein shall remain in full force and effect for the full term hereof unless specifically released and discharged by you in writing. In the event that you and the undersigned shall enter into agreement for any other purpose which shall expire or be terminated for any reason, this agreement shall not be affected by said expiration or termination unless otherwise specifically agreed.

Witness _____   By _____

Title _____   Title _____

Date _____   Date _____

93

CONFIDENTIALITY AND NONCOMPETITION AGREEMENT

FOR AND IN CONSIDERATION of my employment and of the salary and any other compensation hereafter to be paid me by or on behalf of ██████ Systems Company or any of its subsidiaries or affiliates (hereinafter "██████"), I hereby covenant, promise and agree as follows:

1. Ideas, inventions and other information regarded by ██████ as a secret process or trade secret, whether developed by the undersigned or others and whether patentable or not, shall be and remain the property of ██████ and I will take all reasonable steps necessary to protect such information from theft by or disclosure to unauthorized persons, and when requested, will execute such documents as ██████ may from time to time require to safeguard or transfer such information.

2. I hereby covenant and agree with ██████ that I shall carefully guard and keep confidential all information concerning the business, contemplated future business prospects and any other affairs of ██████ or its affiliated companies of which I shall at any time become possessed, which is regarded by ██████ as confidential, proprietary, or private in nature, and that I will at no time, either while I am in the employment of ██████ or after such employment shall have ceased, disclose any such information to any person, firm or corporation, or employ the same in any wise other than for the benefit of ██████ and with its full knowledge and consent.

3. I agree that no change as regards my duties or position with ██████ shall in any way affect my obligations under this Agreement and that termination of my employment, whether initiated by me or by ██████, shall not release me from my covenants and obligations under this Agreement. Upon such termination all records, notes, papers, sketches, drawings, reports, customer lists, summaries or abstracts, or any other documentation, regardless of the medium employed, regarding or relating to ██████ businesses, any contemplated future business prospects of ██████ or its inventions and/or trade secrets which may be in my possession or to which I have had access shall be and remain the exclusive property of ██████ and I will not take with me the originals, any copies thereof, or any notes or summaries based thereon.

4. I further covenant and agree that, except in strict compliance with the terms hereof, I will not accept employment with any person, company, partnership, association or any other entity which competes, directly or indirectly, with any of the products or businesses of ██████ for a period of one year following the termination of my employment. During the course of this one year period, I shall advise ██████ in writing of each and every offer of employment which I receive and wish to accept. Such writing shall be sufficiently detailed regarding the nature and scope of employment which I receive and wish to accept. Such writing shall be sufficiently detailed regarding the nature and scope of the position and compensation offered to me and the identity of the proposed employer. ██████ shall then have thirty days following receipt of said written notification to advise me of its election: (i) waive the provisions of this paragraph 4 only, in which case I shall be free to accept such employment subject to all of the other terms and conditions of this Employment Agreement, or (ii) to insist upon full compliance with the provisions of this paragraph 4, in which case ██████ shall compensate me in an amount equal to the base salary offered by the proposed employer plus any bonus amounts which are not subject to contingencies (such as profitability of the proposed employer or my individual performance) plus ten percent (10%) of said salary and bonus amount in lieu of all other benefits with respect to such employment. This payment shall continue for the duration of the aforesaid one year period or until I shall have received and accepted other employment subject to ██████ approval hereunder, whichever shall first occur. The election by ██████ of option (i) above with respect to one offer of employment by a competitor shall not be deemed a release or waiver with respect to any other offers which I may receive from the same or other competitors during the aforesaid one year period.

5. In the event of a breach of this Agreement, I acknowledge that the remedy at law would be inadequate and that ██████ shall be entitled to an injunction restraining such breach, in addition to any other remedy provided by law. ██████ may also seek reasonable attorney's fees to cover the cost of enforcing this Agreement.

6. I agree that the provisions of this Agreement shall be deemed severable and the invalidity or unenforceability of any provision shall not affect the validity and enforceability of the other provisions hereof. If any provision of the Agreement is unenforceable for any reason whatever, such provisions shall be appropriately limited and given effect to the extent that it may be enforceable.

IN WITNESS WHEREOF, I hereunto set my hand and seal this _____ day of _____ 199__.

_____
Signature

_____
Name: (Print)

Agreed And Accepted
██████

A D D E N D U M

This is a Addendum to ▓▓▓▓ Non-Disclosure and Non-Use Agreement and to ▓▓▓▓ Confidentiality and Noncompetition Agreement.

I, Stuart Shockley, hereafter known as the INVENTOR, truely do understand the importance whereforth a corporation such as ▓▓▓▓, herein after known as the recipient, should maintain a non-disclosure & non-use agreement. Therefore I ask ▓▓▓▓ to respect me as an Inventor and my Inventions by agreeing to this Addendum.

▓▓▓▓ agrees not to use, publish, disclose, divulge, or communicate or reveal to any person, corporation, parent organization, subsiduary, company, or to any person, the information in Appendix A., without the written signature of the Inventor.

In the event ▓▓▓▓ shall cease to exist, be sold, backruptcy, stock market take over, or other means of ceasing to exist as ▓▓▓▓ ▓▓▓▓ imformation, documents, letters, prototypes, will be returned to the Inventor. And that the people involved will still be bound to this agreement.

WHEREAS, the Inventor is willing to enter into such agreement with Recipient, only if the Recipient promises to faithfully keep all information about the Rattle-Buck and all Rattle-Buck products a complete secret and confidential.

1. ACKNOWLEDGMENT OF TRADE SECRETS. The Recipient acknowledges that the following items are the Inventors secret, confidential, unique, and valuable: which were developed by the Inventor over a period of time and cost; and disclosure of any of these items to anyone other than the Inventor will cause the Inventor irreparable injury:

    (a) Confidential customer data;
    (b) Confidential technical data;
    (c) Design, means of operation, materials made of;
    (d) Manufacturing process and the composition of Inventors products.
    (e) Ideals of spliting the Rattle-Buck functions into a single functional product, or any combination of the Rattle-Bucks functions into another product.
    Functions are: (scent , call , rattling , electronic call) Spring means used for operating the device) Operated by a Remote means, Timing means, and/or a Line means.
    (f) Any improvements made to the electronics, timing, remote control, line means, or Rattle-Buck functions belong to Rattle-Buck and Stuart Shockley the Inventor.

2. The Rattle-Buck is the Trademark name for the products. These products are unique and new to the market. Therefore any knowledge of these products prior to this agreement that the Recipient may have obtained either by demostration, in writing, or orally about the Rattle-Buck products or ideals, are bound under this agreement.

3. AGREEMENT NOT TO DIRECTLY OR INDIRECTLY make known , divulge, furnish, make available, or use during the term of this Agreement or thereafter, any Confidential information. The Recipient will not directly or indirectly partake in the manufacturing of the Inventors Rattle-Buck products without a written agreement from the Inventor, given the Recipient the permission to do so.

ADDENDUM

4. AGREEMENT NOT TO DISCLOSE INFORMATION. The Recipient will no disclose to anyone, other than the Inventor, unless otherwise directe in writing by the Inventor any of the items listed above or any of th Inventors other confidential information or trade secrets about th Rattle-Buck Products.

5. Recipient agrees to review Stuart Shockley's invention and ideals for a new and improved Rattle-Buck animal attracting device, and to pay Robert Stuart Shockley a reasonable sum and royalty to be settled by future negotiation or arbitration if it uses or adopts such invention. The Inventor has ownership rights to all new products derived from the Recipient and the Inventors relationship.

6. AGREEMENT BINDING AFTER RECIPIENT AND INVENTOR PART WAYS, the agreement will not terminate upon the parting of ways of the Recipien and Inventor. The terms and conditions will be binding upon Recipien following the end of the business relationship with the Inventor, regardless of the reason for such end of the business relationship, for a period of ten years.

7. AGREEMENT BENEFITS INVENTOR'S SUCCESSORS, ASSIGNS, AFFILIATES, AND SUBSIDIARIES. This agreement will inure to the benefit of Inventor and Inventor's subsidiaries, affiliates, successors, and assigns.

8. INFORCEMENT OF AGREEMENT. This agreement can be enforced by the Inventor and by the Inventors subsidiaries, affiliates, successor , and assigns. Either equitable relief or damages at law or both may be sought for breaches or threatened breaches of this agreement.

9. THIS AGREEMENT SHALL CONTINUE FOR A PERIOD of ten YEARS from, the date hereof.

Accepted and Agreed:

_____   ___/___/___
RECIPIENT (Company Name)   Date

_____   ___/___/___
RECIPIENT (Company Representive)   Date

_____   ___/___/___
RECIPIENT (Individually)   Date

_____   ___/___/___
Stuart Shockley (INVENTOR)   Date

APPENDEX A

Invention 1 : Patent granted on the Rattle-Buck, an animal
attracting device. This device incorporates
methods of attracting animals into one device.
this device may be operated from a remote site.

Invention 2 : Electronic means of operating the Rattle-Buck
and its different functions. The electronics
are not limited to just the Rattle-Buck. Its
uses are as limited as your imagination.

Invention 3 : On going udates, enhancements, and modifications
to the first two inventions.

The first invention has been granted.

The second invention has been filed for patent.

The third invention is currently in process.

I,Stuart Shockley, as an Inventor outside of my skills
as a computer programmer, invent ways that may be beneficial
to ████ This also includes the use by ████ of any of the
three Inventions above that may become a productive source
of income or other value to ████. That as a inventor I
should and will receive in addition to my regular salary
, a compensation or royalty from ████.

Figure 17.

7 SUSPICIOUS MINDS

"There were a number of suspicious things that happened while I was in Eldorado," Stuart commented, taking off on a brand new tangent. "For instance, my front wheel's tie rod fell off while I was driving."

"What? So you lost control?" I ask stunned.

"Yeah, but that wasn't the strangest thing that happened," he said, leading me in an entirely different direction without commenting any further on the first incident.

"I was staying with Doug (Danvers) the last couple of months I was down there. One night he called me on a work night and asked me to get his pot, come to deer camp, and maybe stay the night."

"So this was unusual behavior?" I asked while jotting down my notes.

"Yes. It wasn't deer season, and it was already late in the afternoon. Even today it doesn't really make any sense. I got there about an hour before dark, and a huge camp fire was already burning - actually it was more of a bonfire - but no one was around. So I walked up the road a bit and sat down by a tree. I had my muzzle-loader pistol with me," Stuart paused as if to collect his thoughts while I sat quietly waiting for what's next the same way a child might intently listen to his or her parent reading a suspenseful bedtime story.

"At dark I heard a couple of shots fired. Eventually, here came Doug and John down the road in John's truck, and I got in the back still carrying my pistol" he said leading up to the point when I interrupted.

"Who was John? That's a new name."

"John was a friend of Doug's from New York,

an old service buddy," Stuart added.

"Anyway, a friend of John's was lost in the woods with a 9mm pistol," Stuart continued. "This guy finally made it to the truck – an Eskimo-looking guy, possibly Asian, but definitely not Caucasian – and he gave the gun to Doug."

"So you've never seen this guy before?" I asked.

"No never," he confirmed and then goes on, "For some reason, John is very upset with this guy, and he won't even talk to me. Not long afterwards, John and the stranger leave altogether."

"Don't you wish you could've recorded that conversation they must have had going back into town?" I asked, and Stuart agreed with a nod of his head.

*

"Next thing I knew, Doug and I are both just standing around this enormous fire when Doug says out of the blue, *let's shoot at the fire*, and then he fired off a couple rounds in the fire,

and began acting a little crazy," Stuart
continued, while I am riveted just picturing the
scene.

"I fired off a couple shots of my own
following suit," Stuart continued, "and then Doug
told me to empty the chamber into the fire, but I
refused to do it, and then asked him to put away
his gun. Eventually we left without spending the
night.

"I mean that would've been a crazy thing to
do way out there in the middle of nowhere," he
concluded.

"That's crazy," is all I managed to say
knowing how dangerous those woods can be. On the
other hand, though we'd never been close back in
school, I couldn't help thinking out loud, "I
would have never suspected Doug capable of
something so ominous."

"Yeah you think you know someone, and then
you find out they've slept with your wife,"
Stuart said in reply.

"What?"

"According to Doug, he said it was after we split up, but who knows?" Stuart says in an effort to give me one of those *that's ancient history* looks.

"Yeah, but doesn't that break every single guy code," I asked, "divorced or not? I mean I'd never think of sleeping with one of my girlfriends exes … ever." I replied.

"Going back to where we were, what was your take on what happened out at deer camp?" I asked trying to steer back toward the original conversation.

Stuart continued, "As usual, I was left with more questions than answers. For instance, why did Doug call me out to deer camp to begin with? Why was this strange guy out there wandering around in unfamiliar territory carrying around a 9mm handgun? Why was there an enormous camp fire burning long before I got there? And why did Doug try to get me to empty my gun into the fire?"

"If you were to attempt to answer those questions, what would you say?" I asked, knowing he had probably contemplated this same incident many times over in his own mind.

Taking a deep breath, Stuart continued, "I think if I would not have brought my pistol, they'd have shot me and burned me up in that fire."

Detached, I ask, "If that's so, then who initiated the kill? Who do you think is responsible, and do you think it's tied to your invention?"

He smiled, "Right back where we started, aren't we? Now you know what I live with on a daily basis."

"How do you keep from going insane?" I asked.

"Sometimes you do a little, and then you realize life goes on, and you can't spend it inside staring out your windows," he said, which is about the best answer anyone could give under the circumstances.

"Was there anything else?" I asked.

"There was another suspicious time or two while hunting with Doug down in Eldorado, but aside from that one evening in particular sticks out in my mind," Stuart said. "There was this one time Doug said he wanted to check out my heart, so he took an EKG while we were both under the influence and then asked me to sign it.

"Sometime later Doug came home and noticed his apartment was in disarray and asked if I'd been going through his stuff. I told him I couldn't find the EKG I'd signed so he recovered it and tore it up," he concluded.

"Well that is unusual," I agreed. "You can't help but wonder what his motivation might have been. Why did he ask you to sign this reading knowing you were fucked up at the time, and of course the most logical question, why did he save it?"

*

OFF THE RECORD ... In summation …

"So what's your take on Doug after all of this? I can't help but tell you, I'm baffled by the fact you're still friends with both Paul and Doug. If it were me, I don't think I could be so

charitable and forgiving." I realized I couldn't help the commentary. It was a good thing we're friends and this was not a strictly professional relationship. Otherwise I'd be forced to suppress the urge to voice my opinions from time-to-time.

"Well in the end, I think Paul was used, and Doug was tricked. Don't forget Doug's the one who told me what trick-fucked meant when all this was happening. We were all little more than kids at the time associating with players much bigger and more powerful than ourselves," Stuart explained.

I shook my head in agreement, "I guess anyone can be gotten to if you know the right buttons to push."

"All I know is shortly after all that happened Doug left Eldorado and never returned while I was there," he concluded, certain his suspicions were founded, but unless someone talked, proof would remain elusive.

8 GOING HOME

"Once again, I got a call from out of the blue in October of '96, from an employment office in North Little Rock telling me of a job at *Club Financial* Services, and I'm thinking *this is great, I can finally go back home*," Stuart said, remembering the day when opportunity knocked.

"The first interview went well, and then I went back for a second interview, and the owner walked by the door. The people interviewing me said hello to him and then he left. Suddenly that same smell is apparent. I began to have a chemical taste in my mouth as symptoms began to manifest. I got weak, so I left the interview, got into my truck and drove straight to my parent's house close by. I told them I couldn't breathe.

"Eventually I went back to Eldorado, but my lungs were burning, and for a week and a half I had little or no energy and difficulty breathing. I went in to tell my boss I was quitting, but he wasn't there. A girl that I'd worked with there followed me out to ask why I was leaving and I told her it was because of the chemical smells.

"She told me how her husband was almost killed working for Chemx." Then the smell starts to come from the warehouse across the street where we'd taken the tour. I asked her if she smelled it too, and she said *yes* and suggested we go back inside the office. I told her goodbye and I left never to return," Stuart concluded.

*

"So I went to work at *Club Financial* already knowing I'm going to have to prove myself. They asked me to come in on Sundays, but I managed to get around that. Then this other guy there told me he has everything paid for, and if I played my cards right, I could have it the same way."

"What did he mean by that?" I asked.

"If I played the game according to their rules and kept my mouth shut, everything I owned would be in the clear, meaning home, car,… etc. no payments owed on anything," he answered.

"Sounds unethical to me," I responded back.

"I went on to create an online ACH file processing program, and they told me to sell my invention and *leave it alone,* reiterating once again that I can have *everything paid for* … At one point, I was even told I'd make a nice farmer in Mena, which I'm guessing translated into something like *the sky is the limit*," Stuart went on to elaborate.

"Silly question …" I interjected as I back-tracked a little, "What's an ACH Processing Program?"

"It's a bank file for automatic withdrawal," Stuart answers. "It automatically drafted client's accounts according to how it was instructed. Sort of like membership fees, insurance payments and the like."

"Oh, I understand. That's fairly common these days," I said.

Stuart returned to his previous thought, "But then the chemical smells returned, so I bought a fan to circulate the air so that I could have fresh air to breathe, and then I was asked to stay late to receive a package from UPS, but I got out of it."

"So you had ample reason to get suspicious at this point?" I asked in a somewhat leading fashion.

"Yes, but then I was given an even greater reason for concern," Stuart replied.

I looked up at him staring straight into his eyes, "And that was?"

"I'd gone out for pizza one day during lunch when a fellow employee from *Club Financial* came in and sat down to join me. He signaled to the wait staff he'd like to order a pizza, not noticing I've already started eating from the buffet. He asked me what I liked and I told him

Canadian bacon.

"Then while waiting on his pizza to arrive, he asked me what I wanted to do with my life. In the name of making small talk, I told him about some land I'd purchased and about my invention," Stuart explained.

"By invention you mean *Rattle-Buck*?" I asked for clarification.

"Yes," he confirmed, "And then he went on to say out of the blue *I think you'd make a good farmer in Mena …*"

"And what did you take that to mean exactly?" I asked, already suspicious of what his answer might be.

"At first, I didn't know what to think, but then it came to me. I'd apparently created something of great value to them in terms of how they wished to do business, and they were willing to pay handsomely. In exchange – aside from the monies that might change hands – I was to disappear and forget everything I knew," Stuart answered.

*

"It was then the pizza arrived, and he and the server began joking. Then he uncharacteristically placed a napkin over the pizza and then strongly suggests 3 separate times I have a slice. So I remove the napkin in order to get a slice, and then he immediately covers my hand and the pizza with the napkin, so I withdraw my hand without taking a piece. At that point I refused, I mean what might have been in that pizza?" He asked out loud as opposed to querying me directly.

However, my mind was also racing so I interjected anyway, "Two things instantly came to my mind, one along the same wavelength as you and another you may or may not have even thought about," I continued in an effort to try and expand his thinking.

He looked at me waiting for me to continue, and so I did, "You have to remember, I'm on the outside of all of this, so my perceptions are not necessarily as clouded or influenced in the same way as yours, but considering what you'd already been exposed to, it's logical to think the pizza had in some way been poisoned or tainted. However, he may have also been trying to create an opportunity to grease your palm, especially when he threw a napkin over the pizza while your hand was still there.

"Let's face it, money talks, and if you throw enough of it around in the right places it's almost effortless to orchestrate any number of desired outcomes," I explained as a means to back up my assumptions.

"In terms of simplification, you had created something that was of great use to them that they wished to exploit to their own benefit. As such, they were willing to pay for your invention, but in addition to your intellectual property, they also wanted a guarantee of silence, which is why they kept telling you to *leave it alone*. In this case one might conclude silence was indeed golden," I reasoned.

"That would make sense," Stuart agreed. "You

see, there was supposed to have been a big party that night, some sort of company celebration, but when I didn't take the bait, there was never any party."

"Well there you go …" I responded.

*

"Tell me, what ended your relationship with *CLUB Financial*?" I asked.

"One day about ten employees disappeared into a storeroom and then later came out high. One of my co-workers asked me to write a program for him, and I happen to notice on the side of his computer he had tacked up a quote, *why be stupid and wait when you can have everything now* … which basically went against everything I was ever taught while growing up. It ran contrary to my beliefs in right versus wrong or good versus evil, and was in direct contrast to what I'd learned from my Christian upbringing."

*

"Jumping ahead, at my 3-month review, I got a raise and the first half of my five-thousand dollar bonus, but I told them I didn't agree with their unethical practices," Stuart explained, "And then they responded by telling me *I thought all that went away with the last managers*."

"So what you're telling me is that in no way did they try and address your concerns, much less even inquire as to what you may be referring to in terms of unethical practices?" I asked.

"No," Stuart confided.

"On January 27, 1997 I told them I was quitting, and they asked me to think it over during the course of the weekend. Then on Monday I handed in my letter of resignation and thus resigned, but when I came in the chemical smell was there, and consequently my lungs burned for a week. It felt as if I'd fallen right into their hands," he concluded.

"So what do you make of that exactly?" I asked, "Do you believe you were being sent a strong warning signal, because to me, if they'd have wanted you gone, there were clearly more efficient means to get rid of you?"

"I think they wanted to make certain they could control me, so I guess you could say yes, I was being given a very strong signal," he concurred.

*

OFF THE RECORD ... Convinced he's been consistently harassed and exposed to harmful chemicals, Stuart begins to do two things – extensive record keeping and research on the effects of chemical exposure. Following is an excerpt I discovered within his research. Unfortunately, his research did not include the original source:

Exhibit B. Copied and Pasted from Stuart's Notes

Symptoms of Exposure: *Metallic taste, mouth and throat irritation, gastrointestinal irritation (nausea, vomiting, diarrhea), irritation (nose, throat, respiratory tract), cough, central nervous system depression (dizziness, drowsiness, weakness, fatigue, nausea, headache, unconsciousness), initial central nervous system (CNS) excitation (euphoria, exhilaration, light-headedness) followed by CNS depression (dizziness, drowsiness, weakness, fatigue, nausea, headache, unconsciousness) and other CNS effects, muscle weakness, respiratory depression, shortness of breath, impaired coordination, confusion, difficult or labored breathing, high blood sugar, blood in the urine (hemoglobinuria), blood abnormalities (RBC hemolysis), kidney damage, liver damage, visual impairment (including blindness), coma and death.*

Figures 18. While combing through Stuart's records, I came across a CBC blood panel with Differential readings dated 05/22/96 while he was still working for Chemx. Note the flagged Hemoglobin level of17.1 H g/dL just out of the 11.4 – 17.0 normal range stated to the right. Further research as to probable causes yielded the following results:

What does high hemoglobin mean?
High hemoglobin levels mean that measured hemoglobin levels are above the upper limits of normal for the age and sex of the person (see above normal values). For example, a 19 year old that has a detected hemoglobin level of above 17.7 g/dl would have a high hemoglobin level. Some causes for high hemoglobin levels are as follows:

- Living at a high altitude
- Lung disease (emphysema, COPD)
- Cancer
- Tobacco smoking
- Bone marrow disorders (polycythemiavera)
- Overdose or inappropriate use of the drug epoetin alfa (Epogen, Procrit)
- Blood doping (adding RBC's by IV to the bloodstream)

Davis, MD Phd, Charles Patrick. "Hemoglobin Levels." *EMedicineHealth.* Emedicinehealth.com, 12 Nov. 2014. Web.

```
143-028-0201-0   RESEND      PG  1   03   01 RBL      05-28-96 08:39        KC

             (FINAL)  (T)    | Sex  | Control # | Patient ID | Phys ID
SHOCKLEY, STEWART             |      |           |            |
                             |------|-----------|------------|
                             |Fasting|
                             |      | Account #: 03301525      501-863-7173
                             |------| ENSCO, INC.                        08
2C L                         |Tot Vol| 309 AMERICAN CIRCLE               08
                             |      | EL DORADO        , AR  71730-
                             |      |

Spec Date 05/22/96 Time       |Rcvd 05/22/96|Rpt'd 05/27/96 Time 08:44|Seq#  3390
```

Test	Result	Flag	Units	Reference Interval	Lab
CBC WITH DIFFERENTIAL					
White Blood Count	9.0		X 10-3/uL	4.1 - 10.3	KC
Red Blood Count	5.38		X 10-6/uL	3.85 - 5.60	KC
Hemoglobin	17.1	H	g/dL	11.4 - 17.0	KC
Hematocrit	51.0		%	34.0 - 51.0	KC
MCV	95		fL	81 - 95	KC
MCH	31.9		pg	27.0 - 33.0	KC
MCHC	33.6		g/dL	32.5 - 35.5	KC
Platelets	211		X 10-3/uL	150 - 415	KC
Polys	57		%	45 - 76	KC
Lymphs	32		%	17 - 44	KC
Monocytes	8		%	3 - 10	KC
Eos	2		%	0 - 4	KC
Basos	1		%	0 - 2	KC
Polys (Absolute)	5.1		X 10-3/uL	1.8 - 7.8	KC
Lymphs (Absolute)	2.9		X 10-3/uL	0.7 - 4.5	KC
Monocytes(Absolute)	0.7		X 10-3/uL	0.1 - 1.0	KC
Eos (Absolute Value)	0.2		X 10-3/uL	0.0 - 0.4	KC
Baso(Absolute)	0.1		X 10-3/uL	0.0 - 0.2	KC
POLYCHLORINATED BIPHENYLS-PCB					
PCB-Aroclor 1254	NONE DETECTED			0.0 - 19.9	BN
			Detection Limit = 5.0 mcg/L		
PCB Aroclor 1260	NONE DETECTED			0.0 - 19.9	BN
			Detection Limit = 5.0 mcg/L		

```
     ** Please Note Normal Range Change **

Cholinesterase, S        3650              U/L        1900 - 3800   BN
    **Results verified by**
     repeat testing.
IGE, QN                    30              U/ML          0 - 100    BN

                   USUALLY NEGATIVE FOR ATOPIC ALLERGY          (10
                   EQUIVOCAL FOR ATOPIC ALLERGY       10  -   100
                   PROBABLY ATOPIC ALLERGY                     )100

  **EFFECTIVE JUNE 3, 1996 THE NORMAL RANGE**
    WILL CHANGE DUE TO A CHANGE IN METHOD-
    OLOGY.  THE NEW NORMAL RANGE WILL BE AS
    FOLLOWS:
                   USUALLY NEGATIVE FOR ATOPIC ALLERGY          (18 IU/mL
                   EQUIVOCAL FOR ATOPIC ALLERGY       18  -   158 IU/mL
                   PROBABLY ATOPIC ALLERGY                     )158 IU/mL
```

REPORT

117

9 CHEMICAL WARFARE IN THE WORKPLACE

When most people consider chemical exposure in the workplace, they tend to think in terms of individuals who are exposed as a result of having worked in industrial environments or in processing plants whose methods subject workers to toxic chemicals on a daily basis, but the fact is harmful chemical exposure can occur in any number of ways from direct skin contact to injection, or through the digestive system, and finally inhalation. Breathing contaminated air is the most common method by which harmful chemical agents enter the body, while other chemicals are capable of passing directly through the skin and into the bloodstream.

The first and most obvious question would of course be how can this happen? It's far easier than one might think. According to a fact sheet published on Canadian Centre for Occupational Health and Safety's website:

Contaminated air in the workplace can be inhaled. Air is drawn through the mouth and nose and then into the lungs. An average person will breathe in and out about 12 times a minute. Each of the 12 inhalations brings in about 500 mL of air, corresponding to 6 liters of air per minute, together with any contaminants that the air contains.

Air coming in from the nose and the mouth reaches the back of the throat and enters an area known as the pharynx. The pharynx, which is the entrance to the airways, divides into two tubes, one called the esophagus, which carries food to the stomach, and one called the trachea, which leads down towards the lungs. Contaminated air passes into the trachea which itself divides into two large tubes, each called a bronchus. Each bronchus enters a lung. Once inside its lung, each bronchus starts to branch. The tubes of the bronchus get thinner and thinner as they spread, rather like the branches of a tree. Eventually, the tiniest tubes, which are called bronchioles, end in thin-walled air sacs. Each of these sacs is called an alveolus. Collectively, they are called alveoli and there are many thousands of these in each lung. The walls of the alveoli are very thin and are richly supplied with tiny blood vessels (capillaries). Waste carbon dioxide from the body, carried in the blood inside the veins, can pass out of the veins through the walls of the alveoli to become a part of the air which is exhaled.

Oxygen in the inhaled breath crosses the alveolar walls to enter the blood within the capillaries. Once oxygen has become attached to the blood inside the veins, it is then distributed throughout the body. Chemical vapors, gases and mists which reach the alveoli in the lungs can also pass into the blood and be distributed around the body.

"How Workplace Chemicals Enter the Body, OSH Answers Factsheet." *Canadian Centre for Occupational Health and Safety.* Ccohs.ca, 1 Apr. 2009. Web.

*

Now that the *how* has been established, the next most logical question focuses on symptoms, and in order to adequately answer that question, one needs to know exactly which gas or chemical was inhaled, how deeply and for how long. However, generally speaking, possible symptoms may include irritation of the eyes and nose, cough, blood in the sputum and shortness of breath. In extreme cases, exposure to many types of gases such as chlorine, sulfur dioxide, hydrogen sulfide, nitrogen dioxide and ammonia may severely irritate the lungs.

According to the Consumer Version of the Merck Manual,

Inhalation of some gases and chemicals may also trigger an allergic response that leads to inflammation and, in some cases, scarring in and around the tiny air sacs (alveoli) and bronchioles of the lung. This condition is called hypersensitivity pneumonitis.

Hypersensitivity pneumonitis involves inhalation of an antigen, which leads to an exaggerated immune response. In its acute form, symptoms of HP may include fever, chills, malaise, cough, chest tightness, dyspnea, rash, swelling and headache. Usually symptoms resolve within 12 hours to a couple of days upon cessation of exposure.

On the other hand, refrigerants like ethylene – once inhaled – can cause suffocation by reducing oxygen available for breathing. Thus *inhalation of high vapor concentration may cause dizziness, disorientation, incoordination, narcosis, nausea or vomiting leading to*

unconsciousness, cardiac irregularities or death.

"Safety Data Sheet, R-1150 Ethylene." *National Refrigerants, Inc.* Refrigerants.com/pdf, 1 Apr. 2015. Web.

*

In short, there are as many ways to be harmed, controlled and manipulated – some of which may or may not result in death – through the use of poisonous chemicals and gases as there are names of chemical compounds … roughly about 10 million to date. Nearly everything you touch, taste or smell these days contains some form of organic chemistry including gasoline, oil, most medicines and the plastics you encounter on a daily basis are all the formation of some organically based compound. Therefore, its detectability can be tricky at best, if not downright impossible depending upon the given circumstances. However, with that being said, what is more palatable in terms of the preponderance of evidence – or at least a reason to become highly suspect of those who possess an intent to inflict damage - occurs once the intended victim starts keeping a detailed record of the days and numbers of times symptoms manifest, as well as when and where they arise and who is present at the time of indication.

Then the one remaining question that is all but impossible to answer without hearing from those who are directly responsible is *why*? Why continue to hassle, harass and inflict physical harm on one who merely drew upon his own vast well of knowledge, which he then combined with a spirit for innovation to make the world a better place? Stuart Shockley is a self-professed simple man with simple needs. As such, none of what he created was ever designed with the intention of conquering the world or its inhabitants, much less intended for the use of unethical practices, but rather as a God-fearing husband and father who simply wished to make the means to humbly care for his family.

Instead, he has been forced to live a life fueled by fear and a well warranted degree of paranoia. He's become a man not easily given to thoughts of living a long life, but conversely just surviving each day one at a time while keeping an ever watchful eye out for him and those he cares most about. Life should never have to become that complicated for any of us. It is difficult enough without all the added aggravation, which is why his story is so important.

It is the classic example of David versus Goliath, one small man against a network of power-brokers who cut deals behind closed doors, never again to utter their specific details out loud, and if it can happen to one man, it can happen to hundreds – even thousands – of other unsuspecting individuals who stand in the way of those in control. But like the earth's many hidden fault lines that reside just below the surface, power can have a rather unanticipated way of shifting on occasion, thus reminding us that in Samuel 1:17, David won that battle.

*

EXHIBIT C. This spreadsheet shows documentation of a period lasting approximately 11 months during which time Stuart suffered numerous physical setbacks due to inhalation of harmful chemicals at MedCollect.

HRS	DATE	COMPANY	PROCESS	TASK	CODE
1.00	07/07/2014	MedCollect	Maintenance	DwnLoad changes	CML
0.50	07/11/2014	**MedCollect**	Maintenance	DwnLoad changes	CML
1.00	08/21/2014	**MedCollect**	Maintenance	DwnLoad Clinic Charges	CML-B
0.75	08/21/2014	MedCollect	Maintenance	DwnLoad Clinic Charges	CML
0.50	08/25/2014	MedCollect	Maintenance	DwnLoad Hosp Charges	CML
0.50	08/29/2014	MedCollect	Maintenance	Auto Draft CML- L	
0.50	10/29/2014	MedCollect	Maintenance	Medic Charges	CML
0.75	11/14/2014	MedCollect	Maintenance	Upload charges & process	CMLK
0.75	11/19/2014	MedCollect	Maintenance	Upload charges & process	CMLD
1.50	12/01/2014	MedCollect	Maintenance	Upload charges & process	CML
0.75	12/03/2014	MedCollect	Maintenance	Upload charges & process	CMLBD
0.75	12/10/2014	MedCollect	Maintenance	Upload charges & process	CMLBD
1.25	01/05/2015	MedCollect	Maintenance	Upload charges & process	CML
0.75	01/06/2015	MedCollect	Maintenance	Upload charges & process	CML
0.75	01/08/2015	MedCollect	Maintenance	Upload charges & process	CML
1.00	01/12/2015	MedCollect	Maintenance	Upload charges & process	CML

0.75	01/14/2015	MedCollect	Maintenance	Upload charges & process	CML
1.00	01/19/2015	MedCollect	Maintenance	Upload charges & process	CML
0.75	01/22/2015	MedCollect	Maintenance	Upload charges & process	CML
1.00	01/26/2015	MedCollect	Maintenance	Upload charges & process	CML
0.75	01/29/2015	MedCollect	Maintenance	Upload charges & process	CML
0.75	02/05/2015	MedCollect	Maintenance	Upload charges & process	CML
0.75	02/12/2015	MedCollect	Maintenance	Upload charges & process	CML
0.50	03/25/2015	MedCollect	Maintenance	DwnLoad Hosp Charges	CML
0.50	06/01/2015	MedCollect	Maintenance	DwnLoad Hosp Charges	CML BNK
1.50	06/01/2015	MedCollect	Maintenance	Medic charges & process	DNTM
0.50	06/03/2015	MedCollect	Maintenance	DwnLoad Hosp Charges	CLM BXS
0.50	06/04/2015	MedCollect	Maintenance	DwnLoad Hosp Charges	CML

'CODE' in this case refers to Stuart's assessment of the situation and his reason for taking what he considered to be appropriate action at that time; for example, 'CML' translates to 'chemical medical leave'.

EXHIBIT D. The following represents a formal letter Stuart submitted to his immediate supervisor at MedCollect, Ms. Marry Stsfford, following his latest episode. As a result, he suffered yet another attack shortly thereafter.

07/9/15

Mary Safford,

For the past 13 years I have worked as an Independent Contractor, in the capacity of Computer Consultant, Software Developer and Programmer, as well as Info System Designer, for MedCollect. During these years, I have been exposed chemical smells many times. These chemicals have caused me to have problems with both breathing and an increased heart rate.

I have spoken with you over the years about this problem, and as a result you had Deborah keep her door closed and not come in my office. I am now writing this letter to inform you this is still happening and it's not just Deborah who has vacated during the increased incidence of exposure. During the last 10 months, this situation has occurred 30 times.

Changes must be made so that I no longer come into contact with these chemicals and the smell.

With concern and sincerity,

Stuart Shockley

Convinced he'd been exposed immediately following his submission of the above letter, Stuart reacted same as he'd done on so many previous occasions, by retreating to a nearby Walmart in order to escape his work environment and spend some time clearing his head before getting back behind the wheel of his car to drive the approximate 60 mile commute back homeward.

However, by the time he exited the building, he noticed a truck bearing an interesting logo parked next to his car with the driver standing next to it. They looked directly at one another.

On a day where the heat index in Little Rock exceeded 100° in the shade, the person continued standing next to her vehicle until he left the area, refusing to move even while Stuart snapped a couple quick photos.

Was this person there to intimidate? Or to help? Or was it just an uncanny coincidence? One can only surmise as to which one of the three possibilities is correct.

The door panel's logo reads *Arkansas Department of Environmental Quality*.

Figure 19.

Figure 20.

10 THE PLOT THICKENS

The inability to retrieve the ruling on his original proceedings against Paul Lancaster continued to eat away at Stuart. No matter where he turned, his inquiries were met with innuendo and avoidance as opposed to discovery, which cannot help but build upon the intrigue surrounding this matter.

His first attorney just sat on the case. He later died – supposedly from lung problems – which forced Stuart to seek new representation. After shopping his case to four or five additional counselors to no avail, he solicited a trusted friend's assistance, but when he failed to return Stuart's original call, Stuart was prompted to chase him down. Once again it is a strained conversation. He was told by this unnamed acquaintance "I only know of one other case like this that nobody will take," but he refused to explain why.

Stuart finally went on to arrange a meeting with a Little Rock attorney. Once he was shown to the conference room, the lawyer asks to be excused and then returned wearing his jacket. In order to break the ice he states, "Now that I have my jacket on, it's an official meeting."

*

"I explained my case to him, laying out all the evidence," Stuart said, "and then he told me he would not take the case, but he agreed to instruct me as to how to proceed."

"Did he explain why he wouldn't take your case?" I interjected, asking the obvious question.

"No, but I did do as he instructed. However, when I called him back to follow up, I was told by his secretary he'd gone to Washington," he explained.

"When he returned, I placed another call to him, and I was told he couldn't assist me any further," Stuart concluded.

"Again, I suppose you got no explanation as to why?" I asked as a matter of confirmation.

"No, but I did take Paul to court and won," Stuart added. "Funny thing, following the ruling, while Diana and I were stopped at the water fountain out in the courthouse lobby, RJ (Brown) says to us, 'You're going to need a good real estate lawyer now.'."

*

"Next I landed a position with *Bartman Brothers*, who basically farmed me out as an independent contractor," Stuart continued. "In November of '97 Larone Bartman assigned me a program to print a commission report for *Moss's Equipment* in Mills, Arkansas. After completing the report in January of '98, I kept getting demands from Cherie, who was their individual in charge of inputting the commissions onto a spreadsheet.

"I always pointed her back in the direction of either Larone or Tim Howard – Martman's salesman – because I had no direct authority to make a decision without one of their input. Then I was further instructed to go to Moss's and finish what they wanted and then get out of there," Stuart explained.

"Larry Moss's – according to Larone – was ready to file a lawsuit against Bartman's," he summed up.

While Stuart continued his dissertation, I sifted through his minutes highlighting and underlining, as well as making additional notes for follow-up questions, but it was apparent yet another storm of controversy was brewing behind the scenes.

I wondered how one innocent man could inadvertently stumble into so much intrigue, but then I quickly reminded myself he possessed a talent capable of writing programs specifically targeting a company's individual needs, wants and desires. Computer technology was all still so new back then, and people were just discovering how to make it work in their favor. Thus those who inherently understood the intricacies of this new science became increasingly in demand. While some more reputable companies and corporations remained intent on changing the way society worked and functioned as a whole, other entities were more insidious in their thinking as they focused on writing a new rule book which applied only to them.

"One of the things Moss's wanted was the option to change figures after commissions were assigned," Stuart continued, "I made the changes and put a protection indicator onto them for security. I asked why they didn't just use GL entries to reflect changes."

"GL entries are …" I asked while apologizing for my certain lack of understanding when it came to comprehending his world.

"Sorry I forgot, general ledger. It was

pretty much standard operating procedure back then," he replied.

"Anyway, Cherie said it was needed because of trade-ins and conversions. So in terms of any future liabilities, I then wrote a letter to Larry Moss's with a copy to Larone explaining that the option was added at Moss's' request and that neither I nor Bartman's could be held responsible for any subsequent errors," Stuart explained, as he outlined the events.

*

"On August 4, 1998, it felt as if I'd been sent over to Mills (Arkansas) for reasons that pertained to me personally as opposed to my work at Moss's," he continued, "So when I walked in to the office, the first sentence out of my mouth was, 'How much am I losing by being here at Moss's?'."

"And Cherie responds by saying, 'What does it matter? You're going to get the money from Lancaster.'" Stuart confided.

"Wow! How did she even know Paul

Lancaster's name? I couldn't help wondering in disbelief. I'd never mentioned anything about my ongoing legal affairs," he said with certainty, "Anyway, twenty minutes later, I feel a hand placed on my shoulder, so I looked up and see the owner of the company is standing there. He says to me, 'When this is all over, you need to take a long vacation.'."

"At the time I didn't ask, and to this day I have no idea what he was talking about," Stuart concluded.

I shook my head in disbelief. Considering Stuart had kept his personal matters private, how could Cherie and her employer have even known about Paul Lancaster, and why was Stuart sent to Mills, Arkansas on that day, causing him to miss an important meeting of creditors pertaining to Paul Lancaster's bankruptcy? One could only deduce that strings were being pulled behind the scenes, but those involved were masters at covering their tracks.

*

"On August 5, 1998, I was working on Moss's' programs at the Sheridan, Arkansas office. Once again, I explained I didn't feel as though they should have the updated option enabling changes to the commissions that I'd previously installed, so I added fields to keep a record of the user's name, date, time of entry and changes made to the original. I also made certain previous amounts were saved even if changes had been made," Stuart explained

I couldn't help feeling as if this action was a testament to his honesty. After all, he was not only trying to protect himself, but his employer as well, and that cannot help but speak well of his character.

My thoughts were interrupted by the sound of Stuart's voice once more, "Then on August 7th I completed my work for Moss's, so I invited Larry in to show him the final programs. He invited Connie to join us."

"Who is Connie?" I asked.

"No one particularly important … Larry

Moss's never touched anything to do with computers, so I'm guessing she was just a secretary or someone who needed to know how things worked," he answered.

"I then showed them my complete *Windows* programs and explained to Larry the update could be dangerous if not used carefully," Stuart said, "and then Larry replied, 'For three to four years, until they have sold and cleared out all old conversion equipment, this option was needed to help maintain trade-ins.'."

"Do you think that's conceivable?" I asked as a means to allow for the possibility. "I mean it sounds more than just a little unorthodox, but do you think it's probable his motives were just as he explained?"

He pondered my question for a moment before concluding, "I guess it really didn't matter, because it wasn't my choice what they did with it once my work was finished."

Continuing, "Finally, on August 10th of that same year, Cherie asked if I could post the commissions and interest to the GL. However, I didn't think I should unless the update option was eliminated, thereby making the figures unalterable, in addition to making all future changes with regard to new transactions update the appropriate general ledger numbers," Stuart concluded.

"So did you do as she asked?" I wondered, and if not, then what excuse did he provide in order not to perform the task.

"No I didn't. I had no intention of implicating myself in something illegal," he stated categorically.

*

"There's one interesting sidebar regarding Cherie …" Stuart noted.

"Yeah, what's that?" I asked with notepad in hand.

"She had a direct line to the *Grand Wizard*," Stuart replied unfazed.

"The Ku Klux Klan?" I asked in amazement?

"Don't look so shocked," Stuart

interrupted, "Everyone was back then."

*

"Meanwhile, while all of this other drama is going on, I found out Paul was living in a huge house on Lake Hamilton rent free. It was the Raymond Clinton estate.

"Aside from the obvious, why do I feel like I should know that name?" I asked.

"Raymond Clinton was Virginia Clinton's brother-in-law who of course was Bill's mom," he answered.

I gasped silently thinking to myself, my God, this is ascending. It's impossible not to feel the magnitude of the weight on your shoulders once confronted by realities you'd just as soon not uncover. After all, I'd loved the Clintons for decades. I admired and respected them both. I even looked forward to eventually casting my vote in favor of Hillary come November 2016. I wasn't prepared to hear anything that might dissuade my thinking on that subject.

"When I found out about it, I was pissed,

so back then I confided in the one person I knew I could trust beyond any shadow of doubt," Stuart said.

"Your grandmother," I asked as a matter formality, as I was pretty certain of the answer well in advance of the question, "and what did she say?"

"She said, 'Walk away Stuart.'."

He continued, "My grandmother was well ahead of her time. Not only was she a good business woman who probably earned millions in real estate, she went on to thrive despite my grandfather's death. She even knew *Owney Madden*, the former crime boss who'd been previously banished from New York City and then came to re-locate in Hot Springs, which was pretty much wide open back then in terms of gambling," Stuart said, confiding what had become a well-known fact by the time I grew from a youngster into an adult in our otherwise fair city.

"I remember I protested at the time," he continued, "even going on to say, 'If it was you, would you just walk away?', And she just looked at me and said, 'No.', But then she went on to say something even more interesting …"

"And what was that?" I asked.

"She said, 'Stuart, if you try and change things, it may get even worse.'."

*

"While working at Bartman's, which was below my parent's condo, literally in the same building, it occurred to me that every time a court appearance comes up, I'm either sent to Russellville or Mills," Stuart explained.

"That at least seems premeditated, but just for the record, do you think there's any way it could be considered coincidence?" I asked.

"No, I don't, especially when you consider my dad beat me to the R.J.'s office the day of my settlement only to have left before I arrived," he said in answer to my question. "Like I told you before, it's my opinion my dad cut a deal to take my settlement for himself, but he wasn't saying anything, at least not yet …"

"Then I must admit your suspicions at least seem plausible," I responded, "So what do you do when all these seemingly irrational coincidences begin to fly in the face of reason?"

"I became frustrated and called the FBI, giving them my name in case anything happened to me," Stuart replied.

I shook my head for what must have been dozens of times by now wondering what kept him going when he must've felt so alone. A weaker man might have surrendered to their manipulations, but he wasn't weak. It may indeed sound old-fashioned, but he had things like truth and honor on his side, the very principles that once built this nation. I was at once reminded of the boy that should have died due to electrocution so many years ago, the same one who is now a man still in search of the purpose for which he returned.

Getting back on point, I asked, "What happened next?"

With a pensive look on his face, he

answered, "The next morning my boss came into my office, looked at me then points to the ceiling saying, 'What's upstairs?' He asks?"

*

OFF THE RECORD ... Stuart alluded to having discovered that Paul Lancaster was staying as a guest at the home of Raymond Clinton during the time period when his lawsuit against Paul was still being adjudicated. As a result, he had reason to believe his life might be in danger. But why I asked?

With further research, I was able to uncover an old interview dated June 13, 1996 in which Roger Morris is speaking with Frontline, a companion website to the investigative journalism series as supported by PBS (Public Broadcasting Service).

Roger Morris, according to Wikipedia, "is an American writer who earned his doctorate in government from Harvard University. He entered government service in 1966 as an aide to former United States Secretary of State Dean Acheson. He first joined the National Security Council staff under the administration of Democratic President Lyndon B. Johnson. When Republican Richard Nixon won the presidency in 1968, he appointed Henry Kissinger as his National Security Advisor, and Kissinger asked Morris to remain on the NSC staff as senior staff member. However, Morris resigned in April 1970, when Nixon ordered the Cambodian Campaign.'"

Following is an excerpt of the interview which ran on Frontline as it related to Raymond Clinton:

FL: What are the lessons, for let's say, a young kid like Bill Clinton, aspiring politician. What is it that he sees growing up and how does that shape him specifically.

MORRIS:

Well, we don't know what he really sees because it's the want of American politicians never to talk candidly about themselves, not even in their memoirs, for which they always get a great deal of money. But I think we have a lot of parallel testimony. Shirley Abbott, the writer, grew up in Hot Springs, just a little older than Bill Clinton, and she wrote a wonderful memoir, called *The Bookmaker's*

Daughter, which tells us a lot about being a child in Hot Springs. Her father, of course, was employed by the powers that be and was a bookie in the town for years and years. And her era is the same. The '40s, '50s and '60s. And she has a rather poignant sentence at the end of her memoirs, saying that Hot Springs, Arkansas deconstructs and demolishes the American dream. That it mocks all of the pretense of American democracy, of how the world seems to work, how Americans think their society works and how it really works. All the secret and covert arrangements by which, not just a political system but an economy and a society as well. Hot Springs of course was a very, very strong center of Baptist faith and practice. It was supposed to be a very religious city, full of churches and little Billy Clinton went down Park Avenue to the Baptist church every Sunday morning, with a Bible, with his initials engraved in the cover. And, lived that life on Sunday morning while his parents were attending the clubs and the race tracks and gambling, almost every night, of the week, and coming home with raging fights and a lot of abuse of the mother and of Bill and his brother by the stepfather. So there is, at once, an enormous gap, a kind of disparity between two realities, in the life of any child. Between the reality as one pretends it to be, as you pretend to the outside world, and the real working reality. The most influential male figure, very early in his life, and indeed later in his political start, is his stepfather's brother. A man named Raymond Clinton, who was the dominant figure in the Clinton family. Roger Clinton, Bill's stepfather, was sort of the weak, younger brother who was never, never quite going to make it. He'd been set up in a Buick dealership in Hope, which is where he met Virginia, Bill's mother, and married her, and that failed because he flitted away the company profits in gambling and dissipation and drinking and so on.

The stronger, older brother was Raymond Clinton who had a Buick franchise in Hot Springs and was quite a political force. A member of the Ku Klux Klan and had extensive organized crime ties. He ran his own slot machines, out of the back, not only of the Buick dealership but other businesses and properties around town. Bookmaking and bootlegging operations and all the rest. And it's important to understand that one didn't do that on a freelance basis. You didn't just come into a town owned by organized crime and set up your own vice. You did that only at the sufferance and with the cooperation, indeed collaboration of organized crime, and you gave kickbacks accordingly. So Raymond Clinton, who was a very important figure in the family often rescues Bill from abuse by his stepfather, and is a very dominant financial figure in their, fortunes, was closely linked to those elements.

FL: Somebody said he felt that was the real father figure at that point. The most commanding male presence in his life. So talk a little about what drew Bill to this man...

MORRIS:

Well, Raymond Clinton is a very, powerful figure, he's a

tall, good-looking, very assertive, aggressive man who is a
striking contrast to his younger brother who is weak, and an
alcoholic and seemingly always in trouble. He can't really
hold a job, ends up going bust in the Buick dealership
which Raymond had arranged for him in Hope, coming
back to Hot Springs and going to work for Raymond as a
parts manager in the Buick franchise. Raymond is always
there to take care of this little boy when he is mistreated or
abandoned by the stepfather and often by the mother, who's
out night clubbing as well and who works odd hours as a
nurse at the local hospital. He's very protective, I think it's
clear that Raymond Clinton adopted Bill Clinton in many
respects, saw in him, very early on the political figure, the
charmer, the publicly acceptable face that he became. And
he grooms him. He really raises and nurtures this little boy
I think to be, to be the kind of politician that he ultimately
became.

And then later, Raymond plays a very, very crucial role in
Bill Clinton's life. He is very instrumental, he's the man to
whom Bill Clinton turns in the Vietnam draft crisis, when
he's confronted with this, with the very real prospect of
going to Vietnam. He goes first to Uncle Raymond, who, as
my book describes, goes to great pains to fix this up with
the local board and, staves off the draft. Turns out
decisively. It does enable Bill Clinton to escape the draft, in
a very precise way. And he does this with political
influence. He's very close to Senator Fulbright, and to
Senator McClellan. He knows both Republicans and
Democrats in the state and he travels around on behalf of

his nephew here, his step-nephew really, trying to save him from the Vietnam draft. And then later when Bill Clinton returns, from Yale Law School, to begin almost immediately, a campaign for Congress, launching a bid for Congress in 1974, it's Raymond who is very important financially to him. It's Raymond's house that becomes the campaign headquarters, in a house that he owns in Fayetteville. It's Raymond's money and influence that secures the first of so many bank loans that are so important in Bill Clinton's career. This is the president that the banks of Arkansas made, and Raymond Clinton goes into a bank in Hot Springs, and Bill Clinton comes out with a ten thousand dollar loan which is really quite decisive for that campaign. And he's there also, supporting the 1976 run for Attorney General, and the 1978 campaign for Governor.

Morris, Roger. "Stories of Bill, Interview." *Frontline.* PBS.org. Web. 13 June 1996.

*

Exhibit E. The following are important notes lifted directly from Stuart's journal, written throughout the years of his persecution …

My dad seemed to be doing ok after the second meeting of Paul Lancaster's bankruptcy creditors was

botched up by R.J. Brown.

R.J. Brown suddenly develops heart problems.

R.J. Brown's secretary calls and tells me to go to Paul's bankruptcy 11 7 first meeting.

R.J Brown tells me due to his health he cannot work, and that I should arrange

to pick up my file on this case.

Why is Paul Lancaster hiding? Who is paying his lawyers to represent him? Who is backing Paul? These are all questions that need to be answered.

Why did Sam Strange withdraw from this case? Who was with Bloom Law Firm when he was representing Paul and me against Air Monitor?

The day I faxed a letter to Jack Nickerson thereby forgiving the judgement against Paul, something else

happened?

When I suggested to my parents that I was going to sue Mickey (Lavender & Wyatt), my mother said, "I'm going to get our kitchen first."

*NOTE: Regarding the highlighted section above, Jack Nickerson was the presiding principle over the law firm which bared his same name. By now, it was the Nickerson Law Firm who represented Paul Lancaster in the proceedings against Stuart.

Following the latest twist in the case, R.J. Brown – who had also maintained close contact with Robert Shockley (Stuart's father)- called Stuart and his wife at that time, Diana, crooks and told them to get out of his office. After having been blindsided, later Stuart appeared at R.J. Brown's doorstep in Little Rock in an attempt to get to the bottom of what had just happened, and according to Stuart's recollection, Brown suddenly grew as white as a ghost and looked visibly shaken.

Consequently, they did not speak, and Mr. Brown permanently retired afterwards.

Figure 21. the following pages 153 – 158 represent the Bartman's Systems Contract Programmer Agreement, which Stuart once again refused to sign due to the fact Bartman's refused to make noted changes to the original agreement. Regardless, he continued working for the company *without benefit or protection of a formal*

agreement between both parties.

Figure 22. Page 159 represents the termination

agreement tendered between Bartman Systems and

Stuart Shockley due to an inability to resolve

the ongoing issues related to his work there.

████ Systems
Contract Programmer Agreement

THIS AGREEMENT (the "Agreement"), made and entered into this _____ day of

December, 1998, by and between ████ Systems (hereinafter "the

Company") and Stuart Shockley (hereinafter "Programmer").

WITNESSETH

Whereas, the Company desires that Programmer provide certain computer programming services on an as-needed basis, including services relating to the design and development of certain computer software (such software, including all know-how, trade secrets, copyrights, and patentable inventions, being hereinafter referred to collectively as the Program Materials);

Whereas, the Company and Programmer acknowledge that the Program Materials are anticipated to be integrated into and become part of certain proprietary products owned by the Company, and thereafter to be licensed by the Company to third parties; and

Whereas, both the Company and Programmer desire to set forth in writing the terms and conditions of their dealings, including rights as to the Program Materials; *TAKE OUT*

Now therefore, in consideration of the premises hereof and the mutual covenants and conditions hereinafter set forth and other good and valuable consideration, the receipt and sufficiency of which are hereby acknowledged, the parties hereto, intending to be legally bound, hereby agree as follows:

Section 1

PROGRAMMER SERVICES

1.1   On the terms and conditions set forth herein, the Company hereby engages Programmer to perform the duties defined as discrete projects during the term hereof, on an as-needed basis, and Programmer hereby accepts such engagement. Services may be performed at the Company's facilities, a customer site designated by the Company, or at another site mutually agreed upon by Company and Programmer. Programmer agrees to use its best efforts, at a level consistent with persons having a similar level of education, experience, and expertise in the software industry, in the performance of the services called for hereunder.

1.2 Nothing herein shall be deemed to preclude the Company from retaining the services of other persons or entities undertaking the same or similar services as those undertaken by Programmer or from independently developing or acquiring materials or programs that are similar to, or competitive with, the services provided under this Agreement.

Section 2

TERM OF AGREEMENT

2.1 The term of this Agreement shall be for one year from the date first above written. The actual services shall consist of specific tasks or results to be achieved and shall be performed at mutually agreeable times on an as-needed basis.

Section 3

INDEPENDENT CONTRACTOR

3.1 Programmer agrees that it shall be acting as an independent contractor and shall not be considered or deemed to be an agent, employee, joint venturer, or partner of the Company. Programmer shall have no authority to contract for or bind the Company in any manner and shall not represent him/herself as an agent of the Company or as otherwise authorized to act for or on behalf of the Company. Programmer shall have no status as employee or any right to any benefits that the Company grants its employees.

Section 4

COMPENSATION

4.1 The Company agrees to pay Programmer at the rate of $ 50.00 per hour for each hour of services rendered by Programmer during the term of this Agreement. Programmer shall invoice the Company weekly on Monday for services performed during the preceding week; provided, however, that, unless otherwise agreed in writing by the President of the Company, the Company's maximum liability hereunder for all services performed during the term of this Agreement shall not exceed $ 50,000.

Section 5

OBLIGATION FOR EXPENSES

5.1 This Agreement does not entitle Programmer to any reimbursement of expenses, and Programmer shall bear sole responsibility for any expenses it may incur at any time and in connection with its performance hereunder unless reimbursement is mutually agreed upon and explicitly requested by Programmer and approved in writing by the Company prior to being incurred.

TAKE OUT & add my suggestion

Section 6

OWNERSHIP OF PROGRAM MATERIALS

6.1 Programmer agrees that all Program Materials, reports, and other data or materials generated or developed by programmer under this Agreement or furnished by the Company to Programmer shall be and remain the property of the Company. Programmer specifically agrees that all copyrightable material generated or developed under this Agreement shall be considered works made for hire and that such material shall, upon creation, be owned exclusively by the Company. To the extent that any such material, under applicable law, may not be considered works made for hire, Programmer hereby assigns to the Company the ownership of copyright in such materials, without the necessity of any further consideration, and the Company shall be entitled to obtain and hold in its own name all copyrights in respect of such materials.

6.2 If and to the extent Programmer may, under applicable law, be entitled to claim any ownership interest in the Program Materials, reports, and other data or materials generated or developed by Programmer under this Agreement, Programmer hereby transfers, grants, conveys, assigns, and relinquishes exclusively to the Company all of Programmer's right, title, and interest in and to such materials, under patent, copyright, trade secret, and trademark law, in perpetuity or for the longest period otherwise permitted by law.

6.3 Programmer shall perform any acts that may be deemed necessary or desirable by the Company to evidence more fully transfer of ownership of all materials designated under this Section 6 to the Company to the fullest extent possible, including but not limited to the making of further written assignments in a form determined by the Company.

6.4 To the extent that any preexisting rights are embodied or reflected in the Program Materials, Programmer hereby grants to the Company the irrevocable, perpetual, non-exclusive, worldwide, royalty-free right and license to (1) use, execute, reproduce, display, perform, distribute copies of, and prepare derivative works based upon such preexisting rights and any derivative works thereof and (2) authorize others to do any or all of the foregoing.

6.5 Programmer hereby represents and warrants that it has full right and authority to perform its obligations and grant the rights and licenses herein granted, and that it has neither assigned nor otherwise entered into an agreement by which it purports to assign or transfer any right, title, or interest to any technology or intellectual property right that would conflict with its obligations under this Agreement. Programmer covenants and agrees that it shall not enter into any such agreements.

6.6 Programmer agrees that it shall have and maintain, during performance of this Agreement, written agreements with all employees, contractors, or agents engaged by Programmer in performance hereunder, granting Programmer rights sufficient to support all performance and grants of rights by Programmer. Copies of such agreements shall be provided to the Company promptly upon request.

Section 7

PROTECTION OF PROPRIETARY MATERIALS

7.1   From the date of execution hereof and for as long as the information or data remain Trade Secrets, Programmer shall not use, disclose, or permit any person to obtain any Trade Secrets of the Company, including any materials developed or generated hereunder (whether or not the Trade Secrets are in written or tangible form), except as specifically authorized by the Company.

7.2   As used herein, "Trade Secret" shall mean a whole or any portion or phase of any scientific or technical information, design, process, procedure, formula, or improvement relating to the development, design, and operation of Company business and products that is valuable and not generally known to competitors of the Company.

7.3   Irreparable harm should be presumed if Programmer breaches any covenant in this Agreement for any reason. This Agreement is intended to protect the Company's proprietary rights pertaining to the Program Materials, and any misuse of such rights would cause substantial harm to the Company's business. Therefore, Programmer agrees that a court of competent jurisdiction should immediately enjoin any breach of this Agreement, upon a request by the Company.

Section 8

RETURN OF MATERIALS

8.1   Upon the request of the Company, but in any event upon termination of this Agreement, Programmer shall surrender to the Company all memoranda, notes, records, drawings, manuals, computer software, and other documents or materials (and all copies of same) pertaining to the Program Materials, reports, and other data or materials generated or developed by Programmer or furnished by the Company to the Programmer, including all materials embodying any Trade Secrets. This Section is intended to apply to all materials made or compile by Programmer, as well as to all materials furnished to Programmer by the Company or by anyone else that pertain to the Program Materials.

Section 9

AVOIDANCE OF CONFLICT OF INTEREST

9.1   While under contract with Company, Programmer will not engage in any other business activity that conflicts with its duties to Company. Under no circumstances will Programmer work for any competitor or have any financial interest in any competitor of Company; provided, however, that this Agreement does not prohibit investment of a reasonable part of Programmer's assets in the stock or securities of any competitor whose stock or securities are traded on a national exchange.

Section 10

RESTRICTIONS ON COMPETITION

10.1 Programmer recognizes that it may become familiar with Trade Secrets or Confidential Information of Employer pertaining to the warehousing, distribution and floor covering industries. Therefore, it is possible that Programmer could cause grave harm to Company if it worked for a competitor of Company in these industries.

10.2 While bound by this Agreement and after termination of this Agreement, Programmer will not compete with Company for 12 months by engaging in the marketing, sale, design, development, or operation, of warehousing, distribution or floor covering software or systems. Programmer will refrain from actually performing or directly managing or supervising such activities, whether as principal, agent, employee, consultant, contractor, or co-inventor.

10.3 While bound by this Agreement and after termination of this Agreement, Programmer will not compete with Company for 12 months by accepting compensation from a customer of Company for the performance of services offered by Company to its client base, whether as a principal, agent, employee, consultant, or co-inventor.

10.4 Programmer will promptly notify Company if it receives any offer of employment that involves the activity described above if the offer is received while under contract with the Company, or employment might commence within 12 months after the termination of this Agreement. Such notice shall be in writing and shall contain a complete description of the terms of the of the offer (including the position and compensation offered). After Programmer has so notified the Company, and once the Programmer has indicated its intention to accept the offer if the Company so permits, the Company shall have 15 days to elect:

   a.   To convince Programmer to stay at the same or a different salary, compensation or terms;

   b.   To release Programmer from the above restrictions, but only with respect to the particula employment position offered to Programmer; or

   c.   To insist upon full compliance with the above restrictions.

10.5 While bound by this Agreement and for a period of 12 months after termination of this Agreement Programmer will not knowingly solicit, entice, or persuade any other employees of the Company to leave the services of the Company for any reason.

Section 11

SCOPE OF AGREEMENT

11.1 This Agreement is intended by the parties hereto to be the final expression of their agreement, and it constitutes the full and entire understanding between the parties with respect to the subject hereof, notwithstanding any representations, statements, or agreements to the contrary heretofore made. This Agreement may be amended only in writing signed by the parties to this Agreement.

11.2 For purposes of enforcing this Agreement, all sections of this Agreement, except Section 4.1 hereof, shall be construed as covenants independent of one another and as obligations distinct from all other contracts and agreements between the parties hereto.

Section 12

TERMINATION

12.1   This Agreement may be terminated by either party upon 14 days' written notice to the other party. In the event of termination under this Section by either party prior to the expiration of the term hereof, the Company shall be obligated to compensate Programmer at the rate established herein for services performed prior to the date of such termination.

This Agreement is made under, and in all respects shall be interpreted, construed, and governed by and in accordance with, the laws of the State of Arkansas.

In witness whereof, the parties hereto have caused this Agreement to be duly executed on the day and year first above written.

PROGRAMMER

COMPANY

By Stuart Shockley
      Print Name

By ███████████
      Print Name

Signature

Signature

Date

Date

Address for Correspondence:

Address for Correspondence:

P.O. Box 2228
Street/P.O. Box

███████████
Street/P.O. Box

Conway
City

███████
City

Arkansas   72033
State   Postal Code

███████████
State   Postal Code

ATTN: PEGGY   336-8588
FRM: STUART

December 1, 1998

Stuart Shockley
P.O. Box 2228
Conway, Arkansas   72033

Stuart:

This letter is to confirm the arrangements we agreed to in our telephone conversation on Nov. 30, 1998. Per that discussion, your status as a full-time employee of ██████████ will terminate on Dec. 6, 1998. We will process your payroll check for the week of Nov. 30, 1998 through Dec. 6, 1998, and mail it to you. After that time, any programming services you provide for or on behalf of ██████████ will be in the capacity of a contract programmer, subject to the terms and conditions outlined in the ██████████ Contract Programmer Agreement. A copy of this agreement is enclosed for your review and signature. As a contract programmer, you will no longer be entitled to the benefits provided for ██████████ permanent employees, including medical insurance coverage and leave benefits. For your own protection, I would ask that you return any keys allowing access to ██████████ properties, in particular, the office facilities in Maumelle.

I have asked ██████████ to assess our progress at those customer accounts you have been servicing. Upon completion of this assessment, Tim will define outstanding or future tasks, specific deliverables and estimated timeframes for completion. You will be eligible to assist us in the delivery of these services upon ██████████ receipt of a properly signed Contract Programmer Agreement. A copy of the fully executed agreement will be returned to you for your records. I would ask that any future interaction you have with Gartman Systems' clients be coordinated through us.

I am regretful that we were unable to overcome the obstacles surrounding our current employment arrangement. I hope that in making these changes we will be able to enjoy a more productive and mutually beneficial business relationship. I look forward to working with you as we are able to identify clients and cultivate projects that can benefit from your skills.

Sincerely,

Enclosure (1)

"Providing Automated Information Systems Solutions"

159

11 RAILROADED

Suspicious that he'd been railroaded into somehow forfeiting his settlement in favor of his own father, Stuart is livid. During a meeting at his attorney's office, he informed R.J. Brown he wished to file a lawsuit which prompted the question, "Against who, your own father?"

And Stuart responded, "Mickey Lavender," at which time he was told to *leave Mickey alone.*

Having failed to secure some degree of satisfaction, Stuart sought support from the one place most of us might consider safe, thus he traveled to his parent's home. In a subsequent conversation with his mom and dad, he happened to mention he thinks he should sue Mickey Lavender, and his mom immediately responded by saying, "I'm going to get my kitchen first."

It should be duly noted at that time Stuart's parent's kitchen was unfinished, not even a sink, but more importantly one might ask the question what did one thing have to do with the other? What might Stuart's own parents have known that he didn't … especially as it related to a potential lawsuit he intended to file against a former employer?

Taking the aforementioned exchange into consideration, is it so far-fetched to believe Stuart's own parents might have benefited from a settlement that was originally supposed to have gone to him? He had previously been told by various people who had at one time been intimately involved in the case – namely Sam Strange, formerly of the Bloom *Law Firm* and Trent Kiesling who worked directly with Steve Garver – as well as by several others who more or less operated on the fringe of the case that there was

money there, but despite numerous exhaustive
attempts, Stuart was never able to track it down.
Even to this day, he has still been unable to
uncover the official ruling in his case against
Paul, which his father attended and then left the
attorney's office prior to Stuart's arrival.

In addition, why did the people at *Moss's Equipment* – Stuart's current contractor – seem to know confidential information about Stuart's lawsuit when he had confided nothing? And why did Stuart's work schedule always override his availability whenever an important court date was scheduled?

One might ask how Robert Shockley could have pulled off such a coup. Without help, it would've been impossible. Forget the fact he possessed the same name as Stuart and that any check that passed from one hand to another could have easily been endorsed and then backed up with appropriate credentials, I also think it worth mentioning that during time Stuart's father possessed quite a valuable bargaining chip in the form of

Stuart's intellectual property. Remember, following the dissolution of Stuart and Paul's partnership, Stuart had stored all of his programs and pertinent notes at his father's home, which were apparently being shopped around without his knowledge or consent. At that time when his father asked him what the boxes contained, Stuart answered *the power to change the world*.

As difficult as it is to come to terms with the fact a father might have betrayed his own son, greed became a powerful aphrodisiac that worked much like any addictive substance capable of swaying one's thinking into believing he was doing the right thing as long as he took care of his son in the process, and to the best of his ability, I think Robert Shockley did try to do just that each time a lucrative position suddenly opened up with a good company from out of the blue. However, what he failed to realize was by working with certain other entities behind the scenes, he might have also have been placing his son in harm's way.

Powerful people, who prefer to operate in more clandestine fashion, effectively remain in control by efficiently covering up their tracks along the way, leaving no messes or loose ends left untied in their wake. The fact Stuart's father might have been exposed to such people through having grown up in an influential family in Hot Springs, Arkansas, did not mean he operated on the same level playing field with them. These individuals who control secret societies and pull strings like a puppeteer who has mastered his craft at the highest possible levels are made from different metal than most of us, and they don't abide with being tested.

*

OFF THE RECORD ...

Exhibit F. Unhappy with the fact Paul Lancaster had opted to file bankruptcy, Stuart fired off the following letter to his attorney, R.J. Brown:

Stuart & Diana Shockl

4 Northwood Drive

Conway, Ar. 72033

Faxed 05/26/98

(664-2372)

Dear R. J. Brown,

Diana and I do not understand you asking us to wait for two more years. I would like to

continue on with the game plan we discussed after court on Apr 16, 1998 that Mr. Lancaster should disclose all of his assets, and that I get a judgement. Also as I disclosed earlier, the house on the lake in Hot Springs, which Paul lived in, has yet to close.

 I do not want any statute of limitations to expire.

As you said after court, you think he has something. So do I.

I need the three original documents used as evidence in the trial against Paul.

Respectfully,

Stuart & Diana Shockley

5/26/98

Exhibit G. A sudden twist in the ongoing legal battle brought about even more questions and resulted in the following exchange between Stuart and his representative:

Stuart & Diana Shockley

4 Northwood Drive

Conway, Ar. 72033

Faxed 06/26/98

(664-2372)

Dear R. J. Brown & Crockett,

Why did Paul Lancaster decide not to file bankruptcy?

Possible places Paul may have his finances.

(1.) He had a ring on at the trial. If he is married, check in his wife's name.

(2.) His grandfather who passed away at the first of the year owns Humphreys Dairy, in Hot Springs , AR, county of Garland, on Shady Grove Rd. Paul was probably in his will. Paul's mother, Sally Lancaster, is living in her fathers, Mr. Humphrey's, house.

(3.) The house that Paul lived in for free is selling for over a million dollars. I'm not sure who owns the house. But Melissa Lancaster is Paul's sister-in-law, who is married to Mark

Lancaster. She is the sales agent for the house. Melissa Lancaster's maiden name is Loyd, and Loyd Reality is the broker for the house. Enclosed is a listing of the house.

(4.) Mark Lancaster &/or Melissa Lancaster maybe helping Paul.

(5.) A Possible place may be in Doug Danver's bank Account or his business account MidSouth

Mobile X-ray. When I went to work in Eldorado , AR, back in 96. Doug was in Eldorado, right after I started working in Eldorado he transferred his money from Eldorado to Hot Springs.

He lives in Hot Springs on Shady Grove Rd, but works in Eldorado. Doug also is the one who told me that Paul screwed me.

Please send us a letter of the results of the First Meeting of Bankruptcy of Paul Lancaster.

Again, Thank You for Professional Services,

Stuart & Diana Shockley

6/26/98

*NOTE: After this letter was mailed, Stuart discovered Paul was indeed living at the estate of Raymond Clinton, former president Bill Clinton's uncle. Although Paul's former sister-

in-law was the realtor who held the listing on the property at that time, it seemed unlikely she could have worked out an arrangement for a supposed stranger to live there indefinitely without tendering any rent or signing some kind of lease agreement.

Exhibit H. is another communication from Stuart showing the growing discontent between him and his attorney, due to his perceived lack of representation and follow through with regard to Stuart's lawsuit against Paul Lancaster. However, mounting questions and inconsistencies continued to go unaddressed.

Stuart & Diana Shockley

4 Northwood Drive

Conway, Ar. 72033

Faxed 08/04/98

(664-2372)

Dear Attorney R. J. Brown,

I am writing this so that you will understand that Diana & I are not satisfied with the lack of response and communication on your end. As of the date above, it has been over five weeks since Paul's, First Meeting of Bankruptcy, and I have yet to receive a letter about the meeting or what Paul and his attorney said about settling out of court.

Diana and I do not understand you asking us to wait for two more years. I would like to continue on with the game plan we discussed after court on Apr 16,1998 that Mr. Lancaster

should disclose all of his assets, and that I get a judgement. Also as I disclosed earlier, the house on the lake in Hot Springs, which Paul lived in, has yet to close.

Also the Judge said Mike Hearts was to provide me with results of Air Monitor v. Engineered Instruments, nor has Paul returned my computer programs.

I do not want any statute of limitations to expire.

As you said after court, you think he has something. So do I. It seems to us that your attitude has completely changed.

Why do you continue to put us off I don't know, but Diana and my patience have run out. If Paul and his lawyer have said they would like to settle out of court at the first meeting of Paul's bankruptcy, then I expect that a lawyer whom I paid 600.00 dollars to go to the bankruptcy

meeting to tell me what they want to settle for and to present it to me. Only after finding out what the offer is, can a logical decision be made as to what actions should be taken next.

This simple case has drug on for four years. If the subpoena that I asked you to get, four different times had been taken we would not have to be investigating Paul's assets or hidden assets and the amount of money I should receive would then be obvious.

I need an attorney to represent me and my best interest. And not to drag out a case for whatever reasons they would drag a case out. As I said before you are supposed to get a percent of the settlement for your efforts, and when the case is settled you will get your monies.

I should not have to coax or beg my lawyer to communicate with me.

I expect to know Paul's offer by Friday 08/07/98. As I said before, I want justice and not for anyone to benefit from interest on monies that I should have already received. I also will not put up with any stall tactics or wait to the last minute to get Paul under oath.

I think it would be worth your time in ways that you do not think I realize, that you respond by Friday Aug 7,1998. May I bring it to your attention that this is not just a trivial case.

Respectfully,

Stuart & Diana Shockley

08/04/98

Exhibits H1.and H2. Following are 2 excerpts taken directly from Stuart's notes and dated the same month and year as the previous communication to his lawyer, RJ Brown, which seem to back up his level of confusion and frustration at that time.

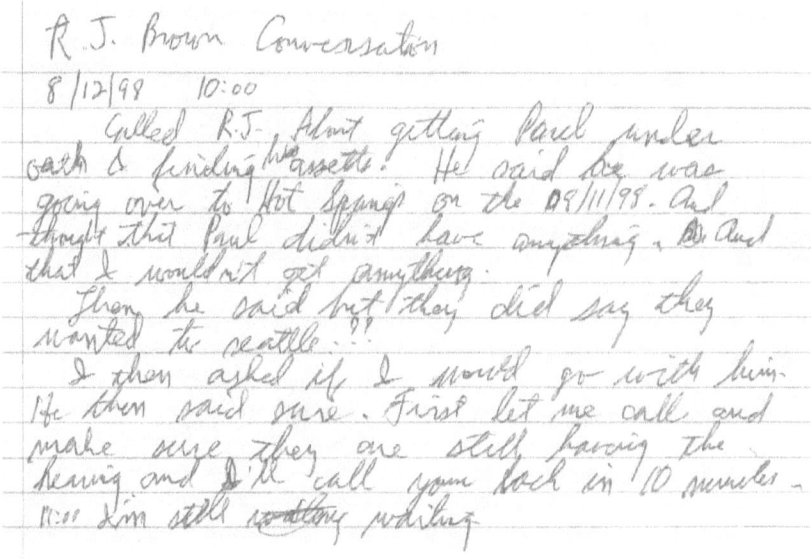

Exhibit H1. (above) & Exhibit H2. (next page)

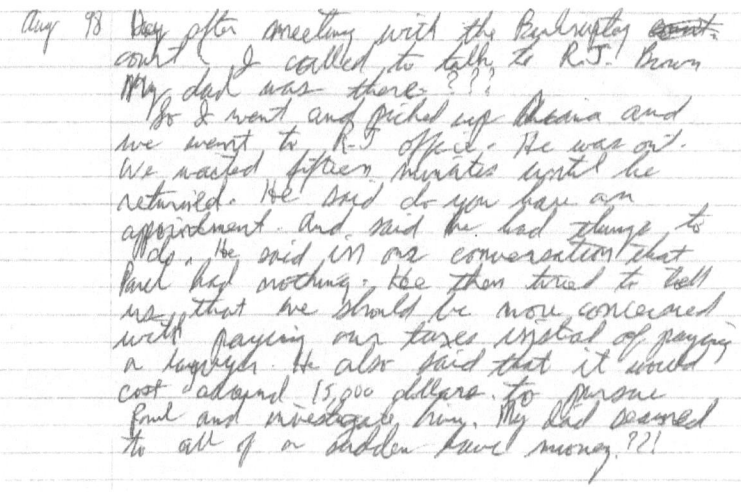

Exhibit I. Following numerous communications and no appreciable response, Stuart reaches out to the Judge in the case for satisfaction. The following communication illustrates this point:

Stuart & Diana Shockley

4 Northwood Drive

Conway, Ar. 72033

Telephone: 09/28/98
(501)513-0264

Hon. Marcia R. Hearnsburger

Re: Shockley v. Lancaster, Garland Circuit No. 96-410

Dear Judge Hearnsberger:

In reference to Circuit No. 96-410 tried on April 16,1998:

Mr. Lancaster, nor his attorney, Mike Hearts Jr., as of the date of this letter have given me the results of the case between Engineered Instruments v. Air Monitor, Pulaski County Circuit Court, No. 947320. Also they have not returned my Computer Programs that Mr. Lancaster has.

The above two items were supposed to have been given to me as part of Case No: 96-410.

The purpose of this letter is to let you know that I have not received either of the two items listed above. Mr. Lancaster claimed bankruptcy, and therefore I won the Battle but lost the War. My attorney, RJ Brown, has ignored my request for the two above items, as he has ignored 90 percent of my requests through this entire case.

Very truly yours,

Stuart Shockley

Mr. Hearts Address:

TCBY Tower, Suite 1524

425 West Capital Ave.

Little Rock AR, 72201

Phone: (501)374-6700

Fax: 374-6665

12 FRIEND OR FOE

Time passed and while Stuart continued pursuing his case - despite the realization of any advantage to having done so - he experienced something which could only be described as unusual. While traveling to his six acres situated outside of town, a large, white ATV pulled up beside him on Highway 10 but did not pass. After accelerating his speed up to 80 mph, he managed to place enough distance between he and the ATV to have pulled off the road until it drove by him.

At this point, he drove back out onto the highway and managed to catch up with the vehicle in question around Paron, Arkansas. It was then he realized the ATV had *Police* on the back, a long antenna and tinted windows. He followed it for a while, and then having made it to his property, he turned off onto his land and began burning trees.

Shortly afterwards, he heard a helicopter and noticed as it traversed low across his land, it was black and white, same as police choppers. Then right before he left for the day, a single-engine crop duster like plane flew over at a low altitude, which was unusual considering it was nowhere near the acres upon acres of delta land situated in the eastern part of the state, which was the only area one ever really witnessed the use of crop dusters.

"What did you make of it?" I asked.

Stuart answered, "In my opinion, the police had me under surveillance, which could've been to either protect me or to catch me in the act of doing something illegal. Who knows?

"Either way, shortly afterwards, I was told

by a co-worker that I was under the witness protection program, but this person refused to elaborate as to why," Stuart confided.

*

To fully grasp the unlikelihood of this particular string of events, one needs to understand the lay of the land. Paron, Arkansas is little more than a *wide spot in the road*, to coin an old southern phrase. An unincorporated community in Saline County, it is situated 17.5 miles northwest of Benton, Arkansas, and known for little more than having produced the popular country singer, Justin Moore.

With a current population of 976, it is a place you drive through going someplace else as opposed to an ultimate destination, unless you're trying to escape the pressures of city living. Those who remain call it home, while those who escape have followed their dreams elsewhere. It is however, a center point between two key cities, Little Rock and Hot Springs. Depending upon which way the wind blows, forty-five miles to the east or west will land you in one or the other.

*

"I went to work for a company called Pleasure *Arts* converting order entry programs to Y2K compliance. As a result, I had questions about certain situations I was working on at that time, and opposed to being properly addressed, I was told *I might end up at the bottom of a cliff* by the manager of inventory," Stuart confided.

"What?" I asked stunned. "What do you think prompted such a response?"

"I don't know. Sometimes, it seems as if all my life people around me have spoken in riddles, as if trying to imply something without really saying much of anything," he answered, "but that's not all. Another told me *a person on death row had a better chance than I did, at least he can appeal*," he said further.

"Interesting …" I responded. "Your notes also state that at that time, you were told not to try and clear your name. Can you elaborate on that?" I asked.

"It's been a long time ago," Stuart replied, "but there was this guy there I used to take smokeless breaks with while everyone else was puffing on their cigarettes. I believe he was from Puerto Rico, and he was brilliant. He'd study a language and not only learn how to speak that language, but also everything there was to know about the various dialects. I think his name was Eddie Gonzalez. Anyway, I really liked and respected him.

"I'd confided in him about some of what was going on, and basically he told me I was screwed," Stuart confided.

"Meaning you had no recourse?" I asked in order to confirm his assumption.

"Right," Stuart agreed, "I think in his own way he was trying to be sympathetic by offering me what he perceived was good advice by implying it was beyond my capabilities to fight it."

"Then one day I was talking with a supervisor about my patent, and he told me, 'you have a nice wife and kids, you should leave your patent alone.'."

"More passive/aggressive threats, I suppose. I guess after a while, it all just begins to roll off of your back, as if someone might as well be saying good day," I commented sympathetically.

"Anyway, after that, my contract expired and I wasn't able to get work from January to June of 2000," he concluded.

*

"Have you ever been to *Pleasure Arts*?" Stuart asked.

"I have actually," I replied. "I used to work for them as an art director back in the late 80's when they were situated in a building just off I-430 in North Little Rock."

"That's where I work now," Stuart interjected.

"Where, at *Pleasure Arts*?" I asked somewhat confused.

"No, in that same building they used to be in North Little Rock off I-430," he answered.

"Really?" I asked, "Small world."

"I meant have you been to their new offices out Highway 10?" Stuart asked.

"I have a couple years ago. I styled a test photo shoot as a means to try and secure some regular contract work through them, and they kept asking me to come back over to donate my time while they made up their minds. That pissed me off. At the time, I thought fuck that, after all my time was every bit as valuable as theirs," I continued.

"I walked into this glamorous building complete with fountains and uniformed security, which made it appear more like an impregnable fortress as opposed to corporate offices, and then they wanted to nickel and dime me to death?" I asked out loud, still unable to hide my resentment.

"You know who owns it don't you?" Stuart commented.

"I know who used to way back when. It was a guy named Steve something or other and he also happened to drive a shiny new red Ferrari," I answered.

"Not anymore," Start commented, "Ted Turner has it now, or at least it's underneath his vast media umbrella."

"Well that explains the upgrade," I added, before moving on to the next topic of discussion, more than happy to let that one fall by the wayside.

*

"Let's talk about what happened to your father," I suggested.

"When he died?" Stuart asked.

"Yes, can you tell me about what you remember from that night?" I asked in return.

"I remember driving home from my parent's place in Maumelle, and I passed an unmarked white van with two men inside, which looked very suspicious to me. For whatever reason, it gave me a really bad vibe at the time.

"I made it home to Conway, and a couple of hours later I got this call from the ER at

Baptist Hospital. My dad had died. I rushed to the ER and when I got there my mom was sitting in the waiting area. She asked me to be the one to identify him. I also remember state troopers being there, and one of them never took his eyes off of me. He just glared at me while displaying no emotion whatsoever," Stuart said in an attempt to describe the scene.

"Did you think it strange your mom asked you to identify him?" I asked.

"Well yeah, they'd been married over thirty years, and he'd died in their home. Nothing was making sense in that moment," he said.

"Maybe she was just in shock. People act differently under those types of stressful situations. Maybe she couldn't bear to see him that way," I added sympathetically.

"Maybe …" Stuart agreed.

"How did your father die anyway? What was the cause of death?" I asked.

"He choked to death," Stuart said.

"Oh my God!" I exclaimed, "On what?" I asked.

"Beans and cornbread, while in bed watching television," he answered.

"I've never heard of choking on such a thing," I stated sounding perplexed.

"Me neither," he concurred, "and Mom said she couldn't roll him over," Stuart added.

"Really? That's strange," I added. I couldn't help thinking had something similar happened to one of my loved ones and I was present, I'd have moved heaven and earth to try and help. I also couldn't help remembering all the times I'd read of people who moved seemingly immovable objects once their adrenalin kicked in.

"Other strange events happened that night as well," Stuart continued, "I was pressured by hospital staff to donate his eyes and strongly discouraged not to pursue an autopsy," he confided.

"What?" I asked in amazement. "You'd just discovered your dad had died tragically and unexpectedly and you're immediately approached for organ donation?"

"Not just approached, but pressured, and only the eyes," he confirmed.

"You know a pathologist could tell if he'd been strangled by his eyes, don't you? The blood vessels burst I believe," I said, which only added to the intrigue.

"And to top it off, the attending physician refused to sign the death certificate," Stuart said.

"Because he didn't want to implicate himself in any way …" I said thinking out loud.

"Possibly, but that's only speculation," he replied.

"I know, it's impossible for us to verify, but maybe an investigative journalist with the right connections could do it," I added while thinking if it were my father I'd have had a tough time letting it go, even these many years later.

"By the way, what happened to his eyes?" I asked.

"I signed off on the donation," Stuart

confided, "At the time, I thought something good might possibly come from all of this."

"I can see that," I said.

*

An unsettling quiet pervaded the room as each of us suddenly got lost in our own thoughts. I realized how difficult it must have been for Stuart to relive such a devastating night. Like most any father and son, he and Stuart had had their differences, but I knew Stuart loved his father all the same.

I also knew where his father was concerned, Stuart had his suspicions that he'd been directly involved in his legal battles with Paul, but at the same time he'd always felt strangely protected by his dad as well, as if he was somehow orchestrating certain opportunities behind the scenes, such as job openings that appeared from out of nowhere. Now he'd lost that safety net, and I couldn't imagine him feeling more alone.

I also thought about all he'd been through

and how for most people this would have been the incident that brought him to his knees, but it didn't. It was just more difficulty heaped on top of an already troubled existence that managed to take its toll on his marriage and the relationship he had with his children, but he didn't break, and he credits that to his strong faith in the teachings he learned in the Bible.

"I have to ask, do you think your father was murdered?"

"I don't know for sure. I had talked with him earlier that same day, because the next day was my birthday."

Stuart was still in midsentence when I interrupted, "Your father died the day before your birthday?" I asked.

"Yes, on May 10th," he confirmed before continuing, "He told me he wanted to get together and speak to me about something the in particular, but he didn't elaborate over the phone," Stuart replied.

"I didn't push it, because we were going to

be speaking face-to-face the very next day," he said.

"So you think he was going to come clean, or at least fill you in on all the facts surrounding your case?" I asked.

"I'll never know for certain but it's another strange coincidence, don't you think?" He countered, "and enough coincidence amounts to evidence."

It was the kind of rhetorical question that didn't beg an answer, at least not in the traditional sense. We both had our suspicions, but for now it had to end there.

*

Looking back, Robert Shockley had once told his son, "Stuart, you have to be part of something," which loosely translated simply meant Robert Shockley believed Stuart needed the kind of mentoring and protection a group might offer him. Following his break-up with Paul Lancaster, Stuart remembered having stored his programs at his dad's home only to later come to the conclusion his dad had gone on to offer them to the highest bidder.

Subsequently, he was contacted by the Shriner organization around that same time and asked to attend an important meeting wherein he was queried somewhat extensively about his work. At that time, even though Stuart couldn't imagine what all the sudden interest was about, he responded well to these men, as it seemed their motives were completely above board and genuine.

As a result, he wound up doing contract work for them for the next seven years while simultaneously the Potentate seemed to have taken him under his wing, grooming him to some degree. Suddenly he was being courted by the organization, which became evident by his having been invited to all their functions even though he was not a Mason. Once Stuart and his wife were even invited to the prestigious Potentate Ball, but having felt it was out of their league, they opted not to attend.

Eventually there was talk targeted at the

possibility of Stuart joining the Shriners, but then someone uttered the words, "We'd expect to be remembered in your will."

At the time Stuart didn't know how to react much less exactly what that entailed. He'd already been ripped off and screwed over in a lawsuit. He told me – as a young man – he'd already seen enough death in his time, and he wasn't ready to start thinking about his own.

I smiled. Having once lived a couple of years with a Mason of the highest degree, I at least had a very basic understanding of what this meant. They obviously saw an intrinsic value in having someone whose technological genius seemed to be ahead of his time become an integral part of their organization. Stuart possessed highly marketable skills that could benefit him the individual – and in a much broader sense – the Shrine.

As a member, they would offer him all the benefits and protections that naturally came along with being part of such a prestigious organization that possessed that brand of clout. In exchange, they'd expect to be remembered in his estate. The Shriners are known for their charitable work – particularly the children's hospitals – but all of that comes at a steep price. Their continued viability depends greatly upon the generosity of their benefactors.

*

"You should've joined them," I said, "They'd have protected you."

"I know that now," Stuart agreed, "but I was just a kid then, and I didn't know what it was all about. I do believe they were trying to help me though."

"Why do you say that?" I asked.

"Because they warned me not to go to *Chemx*…"

*

In the end, it seemed whether a person or organization was a friend or foe depended strictly upon intent. For instance, to show love and compassion for someone means you care about his or her sustainability, and by having done your part, you have directly contributed to an individual's ability to feel happy, healthy and secure in their existence. Thus they continue to grow as a person and go on to make their own contributions toward making the world a better place.

Conversely, when one casts dispersions against another's character, intentionally misleads, manipulates and seeks to destroy someone's health, while continually harassing him or her to the point that the victim must constantly decide what is reasonable versus what is objectionable, then that person must be considered a foe whose motivations are fueled by unsavory desires like a lust for power and greed. On December 17, 2013 Peter Mooring said, "Power is about elimination of opponents."

Stuart's ongoing refusal to take bribes or overlook unethical business practices, not to mention his continued pursuit of his lawsuit against Paul Lancaster and his desire to enforce his patent for *Rattle-Buck,* all combined to make him an opponent to some very powerful people with considerable means. Thus his elimination became necessary through means of delivering just enough targeted harassment as well as continued threats veiled in innuendo, which were undoubtedly designed to communicate one undeniable fact … that *he was not the one in control*. By not eliminating him altogether, they were able to place him in pre-determined positions where he could be constantly monitored while continuing to exploit his natural resources at the same time. As long as he remained useful, he remained safe … at least to some degree.

Once this happens, for the victim it becomes difficult – if not impossible – to decipher exactly who wears the white hats and black hats anymore, because demons are often beautiful, and they sometimes romance with charm. Thus I believe Robert Shockley was lured into believing that what he was doing was the right thing as long as he still took care of his son in the process, but in the end he may very well have cracked the code that lead to his untimely death.

I think it's an undeniable fact there have been many foes in Stuart's life – some who even posed as friends – but there have been allies too, which may account for why he's still here. We can only hope through our combined effort – his and mine – this book might somehow help to one day sort out the good from the bad.

*

OFF THE RECORD: According to the website LIVESTRONG.COM Asphyxiation occurs when the body is deprived of oxygen.

Hemorrhage

Asphyxiation victims often display bloodshot eyes. Their eyes may look reddish with small red or purple splotches, according to ENotes. This condition occurs because of a build-up of pressure within the head, leading to small capillaries bursting in the eyes.

Harklute, Aurora. *"Signs of Asphyxiation."* Livestrong, 24 October 2013.

*

As a result, it seems odd – or at least contrary to reason – to even suggest a hospital staff might pressure a loved one to donate the eyes of a victim of strangulation, knowing his eyes were more than likely damaged in the process of asphyxiation, which of course leads one to suspect a possible cover-up.

13 ROYALS

Eagle Systems, an employment agency out of Dallas, Texas, called one day and said they had a job for me in Edmond, Oklahoma. Thus he began a weekly commute between his home in Conway, Arkansas, to a weekly existence Edmond. While there he lived with an elderly couple he described as *super nice people*, and for once everything appeared to be going well … at least until the last two months he was there, which was November and December of 2000.

It was then the same two concurrent chemical smells began to appear once again, a two-part process of a distinctive sweet smell eventually followed by a bitter aroma that left him feeling weak, disoriented and unable to breath properly.

In addition, he noticed his movements were being monitored, as he had noticed himself being followed at times.

While at *NetSource* there was a regular contractor from Canada named Grant as well as a full time employee named Steve who had always done the backups. Then one day Stuart is told by the pair he must do the backups - and although he asked questions as to why the protocol suddenly changed - he was given no explanation in return, but rather instructions on how to perform the task.

Therefore, he made his way upstairs to the computer room but soon discovered there was a box sitting on a chair in the way of where he needed to be in order to perform his assigned duty. He did not examine it nor seek to discover its contents, but rather ignored the box and performed the backup he had been tasked to complete and was thus never asked to complete the same assignment again.

*

"Then one Friday afternoon Grant asked me about five separate times, 'When are you heading out?'" Stuart confided, "So when I got ready to leave for the day, I went by to tell Grant while he was sitting in the project leader's office that I was going, and he says, 'If you have an accident on the way home, I get your desk.',", Stuart concluded.

"Wow, that's crazy," I said, "Who says things like that?"

"I know," Stuart agreed, "but he was always messing with me. In fact, he was constantly harassing me verbally or trying to play with my mind in some way."

"What happened next?" I asked.

"Well, it so happened on the way home, a man in a truck pulling a worthless 1960's type boat heading down the interstate pulled into me. I looked directly at him and he returned my stare, but then he refused to pull over. I was forced into speeding up to about 80 mph while traveling down the shoulder in order to get around him and avoid a wreak."

"That's insane," was all I replied.

"Then about a week later Grant came into work at about 7:30 in the morning and said, 'Hey Stuart, heck with the baby, take the $40,000.'

"During that time, my son had a child custody/support issue going on while I had a $40,000 judgment against Paul. I asked Grant what he was talking about, but he wouldn't tell me," Stuart explained.

"A couple weeks later he – meaning Grant – was on a plane and suffered a near fatal aneurysm, and that was the last I ever heard of him, but the harassment continued, as I was followed twice the last week I was there. So when my contract ended in December, I left," he concluded.

So that was the end of *NetSource*? I asked.

"Not exactly, actually it became a sort of turning point, though not a good one."

*

"You see, while I was at NetSource, I was

developing a program focused on account modeling, which basically allowed my client to duplicate accounts to assist with setting up new store locations – or so I was told," Stuart explained.

I thought for a moment, and then sought clarification, "So – in a way – you enabled them to create a duplicate set of books, which could prove very valuable in terms of an audit?"

"There was no doubt about it, and while that would have been unethical, you have to understand it wasn't my function to tell a client what they could or couldn't do with a program, but rather to design what was asked of me as fulfillment of my contract. Their ethics was their responsibility," he said while continuing.

"After all, programmers never get audited, but companies do," Stuart concluded.

*

I traveled back to this era in my mind. I had been living in Dallas during that time and remembered a friend I had there who was also a programmer. He – like Stuart – was brilliant, even to the point of being cocky, when it came to his knowledge about this budding technology. Also like Stuart, I remember he had been something of an inventor, as he was always dabbling in something or other in his home studio. Although he didn't possess anything greater than a technical degree, his talents were nonetheless in great demand at that time.

One evening he had attended a design event with my employer and me where all of the Dallas Design District's showrooms stayed open late to show off their latest acquisitions while courting the finest among Dallas's trade. As our small trio ate and drank our way from one lavish event to the next, I remember my friend telling me he wished he could work 24-hours a day, not stopping long enough to eat or drink, because he was that much in demand.

It was such a burgeoning time for that industry. While so few of us – like me – were just trying to figure out how to turn the damned things on, others who understood technology's current and future capabilities were paving the way toward the future. It was a small select group, and they were being treated like royalty while their talents were being shopped all over the globe.

*

"So once it was discovered you could actually write and implement programs thereby enabling a company not only to create a separate set of books, but to price fix as well, what happened next?" I asked.

"Well NetSource wanted to start shopping my talents elsewhere. They'd managed to set up a regular gig for me up in Pittsburgh where they were going to fly me up every Sunday evening and then back on Friday evening so that I could be home on weekends. During the work week, they were going to put me up in a palatial suite and provide everything I wanted or needed at the time. I have to say, it all sounded pretty good to me," Stuart said.

"What happened?" I asked.

"The more I thought about it, the more it didn't seem right. My wife and I were already in a strained relationship and I was having family problems. We were all struggling on some level. It didn't seem justified that I was going to be living like a king while they were all just striving just to get by," Stuart confessed, "So I refused to go and missed their plane on purpose."

"And …" I said in a leading fashion.

"Dimitri – my supervisor at the time – got irate. It was like they had rolled out a red carpet directing me toward a targeted future – one no doubt which would have also netted them considerable profits as well - and once again I refused to play by their rules. As a result, I was kicked off the team – and not just at *NetSource*, but everywhere else as well," Stuart disclosed.

"You see, Oklahoma hadn't been all that bad to me as a whole. Even though on some level I continued getting harassed as if to keep me in line, I was also somewhat protected same as anyone might guard a valuable asset. At one point I was even approached about going into politics," Stuart replied.

"Really?" I commented.

"Yes," he confirmed, "and when I mentioned my past legal battles, I was told 'That's Arkansas, we get around those things in Oklahoma.'."

"Did you ever really consider it - going into politics - that is?" I asked.

"No, I had enough going on at the time," Stuart replied.

"So, you pissed NetSource off, your contract expired and you left. What happened next?" I asked.

"I was black-balled for the next five years," Stuart concluded.

*

OFF THE RECORD: It seems fairly clear to me, the same people who had once stolen Stuart's intellectual property, and then exploited it to their own means - in addition to continuing to withhold pertinent information regarding his lawsuit and subsequent settlement - were the same people who had created a carefully crafted network capable of performing harassment designed to control and manipulate. In addition, they were also creating the opportunities for employment which continued to exploit his talents. At some point, the powers that be had decided while he refused to sell his soul to the devil, Stuart was still far too valuable an asset to eliminate altogether.

Thus they kept him close so as to monitor his movements while networking amongst themselves about Stuart's ongoing battles as they related to his lawsuit, patent and struggles for full disclosure. Had he have taken their bribes and then happily disappeared into the sleepy little town of Mena in western Arkansas, life would have undoubtedly been much simpler, but Stuart had the audacity to choose honor over indecency and has been paying the price ever since.

Two thoughts happen to strike me at this

time … first, it would be interesting to know what had been offered in terms of a monetary incentive, because I hazard a guess it was rather small in comparison to what his intellectual property had really been worth to those who exploited it.

And second, when it came to choosing the path of greatest resistance, I'm reminded it is indeed the road less traveled. However, for a man of faith, it was the only option available and the only one throughout biblical history to have found its reward.

*

A couple days ago, Stuart called me and I could tell by the sound of his voice it hadn't been a good day. He had been reading through the latest group of pages I'd provided, and he got so mad he had to quit. He ended up asking me, "Why me, why have I been made to suffer?"

At a sudden loss for an explanation, I searched my mind for some words of wisdom that might provide some comfort, and I thought about the bible he mentioned so often during the course of our conversations. I spoke of Abraham, Moses and Jonah in the belly of a whale, and then I mentioned Jesus and his disciples telling him good men are often forced to suffer for the greater good of mankind but then go on to experience greatness within the process. I told him to think of all the good they did and the teachings they left us with, lessons we still enjoy today.

Then I told him I'd like to believe all of this suffering on your part will one day lead to good as well - not just for you - but for others like you who have been persecuted for trying to make the world a better place.

*

According to PR Newswire … some background on NetSource:

About The XXXXXXXX Group, Inc.

The XXXXXXXX Group, Inc. (Nasdaq: XXXX) (www.XXXXXXX XXX.com) is an

e-solutions provider that delivers consulting and highly specialized solutions

 to strategize, build, manage, and protect sophisticated i
nformation systems

 and their underlying networked infrastructure. The growin
g XXXXXX team of

 information technology professionals enables organization
s to confidently take

 advantage of the e-business opportunities created by the
explosive growth in

 Internet, extranet, and business-to-business electronic c
ommerce.

    XXXXXXX is a trademark of The XXXXXX Group, Inc.

"The XXXXXXXX Group to Establish E-Solutions Deve
lopment Center in XXXXXXX; Center Expected to Ad
d 250 Technical Jobs Over Next Two Years." *PR New
swire.* Web.

XXXXXXXXX - Confidential

14 PAYBACK'S A BITCH

"I wound up going back to Lavender & Wyatt for a second time - but considering what had happened to me the first time - I wasn't happy there. So I went to a recording studio to record animal sounds for my patented call, and when I got back, Mickey fired me, but in all honesty I probably deserved it."

"Probably so," I agreed, "but it wouldn't have worked out anyway. You know that, but I guess you went there, because you needed a job, and I get that," I said sympathetically.

"But as a result, I was virtually black-balled worldwide. The only work I was able to get was in places where my programs were easily ripped off - or even worse - finishing up work on incomplete programs that had already been stolen from me down in Eldorado," Stuart continued.

"I had seventeen years' AS400 experience and had accomplished a lot, including the search process used all over the internet, and yet I couldn't get a job anywhere in the state unless it was to their advantage. Consequently, I think it's fair to say employment agencies like Snelling & Snelling, Employment World, Executive Recruiters, Seatec and more did not represent me fairly according to my expertise.

"So how did you spend your time?" I asked.

"I began writing things down, details covering the entire span of my professional career and the inventions I'd created. I wrote down suspicions, coincidences and anything else that appeared out of the ordinary, and I began sending letters," Stuart replied.

*

Exhibit J. Following is a letter Stuart wrote and subsequently mailed to Judge Marcia R. Hearnsburger who adjudicated the case between Stuart and Paul Lancaster following the break-up of their partnership. In addition to expressing

his continued frustration over not being able to

track down the court's ruling, he also asked for

the return of his intellectual property and

voiced his discontent at having to battle his own

legal representation.

Stuart & Diana Shockley

4 Northwood Drive

Conway, AR.   72033

Telephone: 10 / 08/ 98
(501) 513-0264

Hon. Marcia R. Hearnsburger,

Re: Shockley v. Lancaster, Garland Circuit No. 96-410

Dear Judge Hearnsberger:

   Thank you, for promptly sending the results of case No. 96-410. Even though this is not what I was asking for, I do appreciate your immediate response.

   The case against Mr. Lancaster went to trial because according to exhibit 1, page 2 line starting with Installment 4: has never been given to me. And during questioning,

Mike Hearts asked me about the results, and I replied," Mike you never gave me the Results of case 94-7320, and when I asked you for the results Mike, you told me that I would have to pay you to find the file, so you could give me the result".

I am pretty sure, Judge Hearnsberger asked Mr. Hearts to give me the results of the case 94-7320. This is what I was referring to in my fax on Oct 7, 1998 because I have never received the results. I have been told by two sources there was a sizable amount of money in the settlement of case 94-7320 Pulaski County Circuit Court.

Also in the case against Mr. Lancaster, Mr. Lancaster was asked about my programs, by R.J. Brown when RJ asked and showed Mr. Lancaster documentation of the Software I wrote. Mr. Lancaster still has a copy, as well as the diskettes to my software. This I would like to have back.

I have included two letters, one that I sent on 08/04/98, and one that I have yet to send to R.J. Brown. I have had to fight with my lawyer the whole time. May I ask you as to what actions I should take toward getting to the truth?

Very truly yours,

Stuart Shockley

Mr. Hearts Address:

TCBY Tower, Suite 1524

425 West Capital Ave.

Little Rock AR, 72201

Phone: (501) 374-6700

Fax: 374-6665

Exhibit K. This letter was sent to the attorney who represented Stuart in his action against Paul Lancaster. It outlines in point-by-point fashion, sixteen reasons why Stuart and his wife (Diana)

are discontent with their representation and then

documents exactly what is happening at during

time.

A copy is forwarded to the Hon. Judge Marcia

Hearnsberger.

Stuart & Diana Shockley

4 Northwood Drive

Conway, AR.   72033

Faxed 09/17/98

(664-2372)

R. J. Brown,

I am writing this so that you, R.J. Brown, will understand that Diana & I are not satisfied with the outcome of this lawsuit against Paul Lancaster.

Diana and I do not understand why you sent Crockett to Paul Lancaster's Bankruptcy First

Meeting!

1A. Much more than this letter. See attached Letter 1A.

1. First of all, I paid six hundred dollars for you to go and represent me in Paul Lancaster's

First Bankruptcy Meeting and you sent your then partner, Richard Crockett.

2. I feel like I should have been at the meeting but was told by you that I did not need to be present at the meeting. Plus I think I was intentionally sent out of town the day of the First Meeting. I feel this way because I asked a person where I worked that day," What am I losing by being here today?" and his response was, "It does not matter, you have plenty of money." Hmm what a response from someone who should not have even known what my question meant, because I had not told anyone about what I was missing that day.

3. Mr. Crockett told my wife Diana that Paul wanted to settle at the First Bankruptcy Meeting.

So why have you never found out what he was offering?

4. I have asked you about five times why you have never given me a letter as to what took place in Paul Lancaster's Bankruptcy First Meeting.

5. Why did you and Crockett split into separate Corporations directly after the First Meeting?

Is this a tactic to protect???

6. Again I was at a client's office near the time of Paul's second bankruptcy meeting. And agai I said " What am I losing by being here today?" and the reply was, "What does it matter? You are getting your money from Lancaster." I said, "Do you know Lancaster?" And they said, "I didn't say Lancaster, did I say Lancaster?" About an hour later, a major player of the company came to where I was working at a computer terminal and said, "After this is all over you need to take a long vacation." Hmm what does this mean?

7. You botched this case up by not taking depositions and not responding to the first meeting in time. Also by filing for a sixty-day continuance, and then never questioning Paul under oath as well as never checking out my leads as to where the money may have been hidden.

8. If you would have taken the depositions, we would know about the monies involved as well as where it went.

9. This should have been a very simple case. Why did it take four years to process? And a lawyer died. Not that it had anything to do with this case.??? But what are you hiding with this case?

10.   Why was my dad there early on the morning of 08/14/98?

11.   Also, the Judge said Mike Heart was to provide me with the results of Air Monitor v. Engineered Instruments, and that Paul was to return my computer programs. I wrote Judge Hearnsburger asking that she help get the results and my programs. She said that it is out of her district, and I should talk to my lawyer.

12. I have told you that I do not want any statute of limitations to expire.

13. On our drop in meeting on 08/14/98 in which you were supposed to have given us the results of the second meeting, you tried to discourage Diana and I, as well as degrade me by saying the sentence, "Who is involved with drugs, laundering of money, and whatever else you negatively said?"

I have not been involved in these, except for a habit I overcame. So was that a threat?? Also why did you say that it could cost me up to 15 thousand dollars to pursue this case. And finally, you continually wanted me to tell you who had told me that there was a lot of money in the case 94-7320 that was supposed to be mine. WHAT IS WRONG WITH THIS PICTURE?????

14. I have nothing to hide, and I am willing to go to all lengths to get at the truth, because my family and I are the ones who have suffered at the expense of others.

15. Why did your attitude change after the court case?

16. Why you continue to put us off I don't know. but Diana and my patience has run out. If Paul and his lawyer have said they would like to settle out of court at the first meeting of Paul's' bankruptcy, then I expect that a lawyer to whom I paid 600.00 dollars to attend the bankruptcy meeting, to tell me what they want to settle for and then present it to me. Only after finding out what the offer is, can a logical decision be made as to what actions should be taken next.

*

OFF THE RECORD ... The anomalies associated with this case are almost too endless to delineate; however, the above represents a partial list of curious items of interest as noted by Stuart, himself, at the time all of this was happening. It appears evident to me – aside from the fact Stuart and his then wife, Diana – were not only being represented poorly, but also being manipulated by others who chose to remain anonymous. Furthermore, it seems unconscionable to me that in a world who champions 'Freedom of Information', that a plaintiff in a lawsuit is still unable to discover the ruling in the very case he initiated against a former business partner.

15 IDLE MINDS

Suddenly with too much time on his hands, the quest for information became an obsession, especially when Stuart continued to run into brick walls. With no job or money coming in, a marriage on the rocks and strained relationships with his two teenage children, he had little left to lose by going on a fact-finding mission.

Thus in January of 2001 – following a considerable effort to locate him – Stuart called his former legal representative, R.J. Brown, and he acted as if he didn't remember anything. Was he in hiding? If not, then one could only conclude his memory of the events had somehow been erased, which seemed highly unlikely.

In addition, Paul could not be found

through the use of traditional means in terms of his social security number or phone records. One day – while he was at the courthouse looking up records on his own property – Stuart had some extra time on his hands and decided to enter Paul Lancaster's name in the search base. The search yielded a $125,000 transaction, despite the fact he had claimed bankruptcy. He was listed in conjunction with a lady named Dianne Johnson

At the time, Stuart wondered if that was what R.J. Brown had meant when he had made the comment to him and his wife, Diana, at the courthouse immediately following session, "You're going to need a good real estate lawyer."

At any rate, in February of 2001, Stuart decided to call Dianne Johnson to inquire as to how to get in touch with Paul and was told she had a restraining order against Paul. She also said he was a con, and that he'd robbed her of over $200,000. Suddenly it looked as if either Paul had been a part of something – some kind of side agreement – or he had been used to accomplish a nefarious plan that had been concocted by others.

It has been Stuart's opinion that Paul and his attorney, Mike Hearts, had cut a deal with his own lawyer, R.J. Brown. He believed this back then - and still continues to believe it today - because despite having once been told otherwise, Mr. Brown went on to tell Stuart and his wife Paul did not wish to settle and then advised them to wait a couple years before pursuing the case any further.

In addition, he believed Paul eventually claimed bankruptcy to conceal his settlement in the *Air Monitor* case - which had been held out in California - and then went on to hide those funds through Dianne Johnson. Paul had married and then subsequently divorced Dianne the same month the case with *Air Monitor* was settled, presumably to get his hands on the money, which would account for Dianne's disdain for her former husband. It's also conceivable to believe the advice to *wait a couple of years* could have played out well for

Stuart's opponents in terms of causing any further action to fall prey to the Statute of Limitations.

*

As a matter of record, Dianne Johnson was once neighbor to Mark Lancaster, Paul's brother, and married to Doug Johnson during that same time. Doug Johnson had once been one of Paul's best friends. Paul and Dianne got married in May of 1999 and by October of that same year Dianne claimed her husband had taken her for over $200,000 – which was the same month the lawsuit against *Air Monitor* ended with non-prejudice. They eventually divorced in February of 2001. Oddly enough, Stuart's continued records search failed to yield a marriage license was ever filed in Hot Springs for Paul Lancaster and Dianne Johnson.

Stuart suspected that beginning with the end of the case against *Air Monitor*, that Paul Lancaster, Mike Hearts and Paul's wife at that time, Dianne, were hiding money by funneling it into real estate transactions. Records included a property Dianne Johnson once lived in having sold for $118,000 cash.

Stuart had become familiar with the inner-workings of real estate and how it worked from a young age. After all, his grandmother had once been a well-respected, successful realtor and his father had gone on to follow in her footsteps. The nature of the facts surrounding his investigation was beginning to suggest it had become an excellent way in which to launder money.

*

A year ago, Stuart decided to run a U.S. search on himself in terms of uncovering all available public records but was told it had to be redone, because there were items listed that shouldn't be there. Then in January, he decided to run a similar search on his mom and discovered there were 110 real estate transactions listed on the building where his mother (and previously his father) lived at that time, which he sees online;

however, when the official report is emailed to him, that number had been reduced to only four. Details were sketchy; however, one name kept popping up repetitiously, *Deltic Timber*, headquartered out of Eldorado, Arkansas.

*

On the last night Stuart saw his father alive, Robert Shockley had his son pull up a particular site on his computer. Situated just off Carpenter Dam Road in Hot Springs, Arkansas, was a new high-end residential development, a gated community complete with security called *Red Oak Ridge*.

He pointed at the map and said to Stuart, "There, that's where you want to be." It should be further noted *Red Oak Ridge* is owned by the *Deltic Timber Corporation*.

*

After having uncovered the real estate transaction concerning Paul at the courthouse, as well as having been told about the $200,000 he had allegedly stolen from his wife of six months,

Stuart found out where Paul was living and decided to do an online property search in an attempt to discover who he was currently living with, but the search kept yielding an error.

Frustrated, he called the number listed on the site and was told they'd fix it; however, this did not occur. Therefore, he called back the following day and was told they should have it up within two hours. Stuart waited a total of four hours before he placed yet another call only to be told that Arkansas had been *discontinued*.

That property in question was at 929 Airport Road, Hot Springs, Arkansas 71913, the estate attributed to Raymond Clinton.

*

In the meantime, Stuart was receiving numerous daily telephone calls which ended in hang-ups. He also suffered numerous flat tires during a seven year period – which fell in this same timeframe – estimated somewhere between a number of 25-40, usually due to an embedded nail about 2 ½" in length. He was constantly receiving mail that had previously been opened. Even his letter from the *United States Trademark and Patent* office had been tampered with prompting him to register an official complaint about the ongoing violations to the Maumelle, Arkansas post office.

*

After speaking with the U.S. Patent office for four straight days, a Mrs. Day in that office told Stuart his patent had been abandoned on March 22, 1998 and then agreed to mail back to him copies of his patent. He asked himself at that time, *what was the statute of limitations?*

He then took his disclosure letter to the post office and asked for a certificate of mailing for his records. He subsequently watched as the clerk filled out the label backwards, which would have sent it back to his own post office box. Stuart began to seal the envelope while simultaneously showing the attendant how to seal it so that it could not be tampered with by bending in the corners before sealing it, and then the clerk said, "Oh! I filled this out wrong," and then proceeded to fill a new label out correctly.

Stuart paid his bill and then asked if he could have his package back, but the postal clerk informed him that *he* had to be the one to mail it and then guaranteed Stuart it would go out in the 12 p.m. mail. Stuart couldn't help wondering to himself … *just how much his patent was truly worth.*

Then on March 27th he received his patent information from Mrs. Day from the Patent and Trademark office in Washington D.C. only to discover it had been previously opened and some of the contents were missing. One day later Stuart traveled to his post office box where he discovered a brochure from IBM wherein all three tabs meant to secure it shut had been busted open. Who was behind all of this and why?

The United States Post Office is a branch of the federal government, and therefore tampering with someone's mail is a federal crime.

General access can only be obtained from the inside, therefore it's reasonable to suspect whoever was involved had the kind of influence that could only come from a very high level.

*

OFF THE RECORD: A very dear friend told me once long ago, "Time can either be your friend or your enemy. At that time he was a practicing psychologist who was counseling my mother, father and me on how to cope with our grief following the tragic loss of my parent's only son and my brother.

Dr. Stanley could be particularly compassionate, as well as understanding due to the fact he had lost his own son in a drowning accident not that long before. Despite the old adage, 'time heals all wounds' he instinctively knew some wounds are never quite healed. They made fade in appearance and crust over a little bit, but an injury that is so severe never truly mends.

And so it goes … over the course of time

one learns how to more or less cope and then something – perhaps a new piece of information, another piece of the puzzle – acts as a triggering mechanism opening up old wounds, and once again time becomes the enemy as too many questions continue to go unanswered. As a result, pressures begin to mount.

But for a patient man, time can also be a friend once you decide to content yourself by quietly remaining in the background while keeping an ever watchful eye on what's going on around you while continuing to take notes in an effort to maintain a running record. Then in an instant, tables are turned once the victim - like the seasoned hunter who stalks his prey over vast distances – seizes just the right time to exercise his advantage through the telling of his story, thus calling out the names of all who have done him wrong.

*

Following is some information on Deltic Timber Corporation as taken from the company's website:

Deltic Timber Corporation is a natural resources company focused on the ownership and management of timberland. The Company owns 530,000 acres of timberland, operates two sawmills, and is engaged in real estate development. Headquartered in El Dorado, Arkansas, the Company's operations are located primarily in Arkansas and north Louisiana. Deltic stock is listed on the New York Stock Exchange under the symbol DEL.

Deltic's history dates back to 1907 when C.H. Murphy, Sr. began investing in timberland and built a sawmill in south Arkansas. Mr. Murphy continued to acquire land through the years and in September 1952; he transferred his land holdings to the Murphy Corporation in exchange for common stock. With this transaction, Deltic Farm & Timber, Inc. was formed as a wholly-owned subsidiary of Murphy Oil. In 1971, Deltic entered the lumber manufacturing business with the construction of a sawmill in Ola, Arkansas. A second mill in Waldo, Arkansas, was added in 1974. In 1989, Deltic began marketing residential property in Chenal Valley, its real estate development in west Little Rock, Arkansas. During 1996, construction began on the Company's medium density fiberboard joint venture in El Dorado, Arkansas. In late 1996, Murphy Oil declared a stock dividend to spin off Deltic Farm & Timber, which was reincorporated as Deltic Timber Corporation.

Deltic's real estate segment consists of three development projects - Chenal Valley, Chenal Downs, and Red Oak Ridge. Chenal Valley, located in west Little Rock, Arkansas, is the Company's primary real estate development. It is a 4,800-acre upscale planned community, centered around two Robert Trent Jones, Jr. designed golf courses. Chenal Downs, located just outside of Chenal Valley, is a 400-acre equestrian development. Red Oak Ridge is an 800-acre upscale development located in Hot Springs, Arkansas.

"Deltic Home Page." *Deltic.com.* Web.

16 The New Normal

During the time he was unemployed, things became increasingly strained at home, therefore, Stuart and his wife, Diana, separated and he then moved into his parent's condo at a high rise in Maumelle, Arkansas. For a period of time, he became despondent and lacked motivation to do much of anything until he decided to take up running, which is when he met what he called his guardian angel, and elderly woman who lived in the same building. Her name was Diane Stephenson, and she was President of the Arthritis Foundation.

Over time, they got to know one another and became fast friends. An unlikely pair, they were separated in age by more than twenty years, but true friendship knows no boundaries once camaraderie is established. It was she who relied upon her extensive connections to find Stuart work when he needed it most, thereby once again replacing despair with hope as he then went to work for *MedCollect*.

As of May 15th 2003 until present, Stuart's been employed by MedCollect, which operates out of the former *Pleasure Arts* building located just over the I-430 bridge which spans the Arkansas River entering North Little Rock. By now he's grown tired of being harassed by the same chemicals smells, so he began documenting the incidents (see page 91 for the table) while at the same time carefully noting other pertinent details. Certain patterns emerged, for instance, most of the time the secretary left around 11 a.m. and then the president, Mark Oliver, takes a walk by Stuart's door on his way out prior to each new episode. Then he smells the chemical – but it's too late by then – because he's already inhaled it.

The chemicals themselves are distinguishable according to their distinct scents. The first is always sweet subsequently followed by an increasingly bitter aroma.

More than once he's approached his direct supervisor, Mary *Safford,* regarding the chemicals (see page 100 to see his latest letter to that effect) as a means to lodge an official complaint, but to date he has not gained any significant satisfaction by way of making his working environment more equitable.

Another co-worker by the name of Deborah has been warned about the chemicals from someone outside of her work environment - and as a result - has been told to *keep her door closed*. Once she told Stuart in confidence *my uncle tells me what to do*.

In an attempt to take a proactive approach, Stuart now operates a filtered fan on his desk to help aid in air circulation, and immediately upon exposure, he exits the building to a place where he can breathe clean air. Recently, on several such occasions, he has noticed an ambulance parked adjacent to where he works in an abandoned lot with two individuals inside. This gives him an eerie feeling.

Upon this revelation, I asked him hypothetically, "What do you think would be the neatest, cleanest and easiest way to get rid of a body?"

He peered back at me without saying a word, so I said it for him, "An ambulance. Nobody – except for some ambulance-chasing lawyer – tracks one down to see who's inside."

*

Stuart has long since forgiven the debt between himself and Paul Lancaster, thus valuing his friendship above all else. So he recently told Paul – who had since been made aware of Stuart's suspicions in relation to chemical harassment – that he hadn't been exposed for about three months since having done an online search for companies who inspect workplace environments while he was still at work, and then incidents on both June 1st and June 3rd of this year were very strong, as if their potency had been intentionally doubled.

Stuart managed to retreat to a nearby facility, Hawk Bank, which is owned by the same company as his employer. He instantly noticed the smell there as well and was told by a teller that *Baudreus is expanding and painting* in an attempt to account for the smell.

It should be noted that Baudreus is an Italian restaurant situated across from the bank's drive-thru window approximately 30-40 feet away and therefore not located directly adjacent to the bank itself, which begs the question, *why then would the chemicals still be evident at the bank?* Unable to make any sense of the situation, Stuart returned to work.

However, back at work, he couldn't breathe so he traveled home to where he still felt incapacitated for the next three hours. Now weak and lethargic, he continued to have difficulty breathing.

*

Then on June 2nd the entryway to the offices
had a cart full of boxes containing statement
forms. The smell emanating from inside them was
the harsher one – the bitter smell – and it was
very strong. One sniff and Stuart labored to hold
his breath while entering the door code in an
effort to make his way through the entry area.

Between the dates of June 2nd and 4th, he'd
had to pass through that same foyer at work about
twenty times before departing for a weekend. Each
time he was continuously forced to hold his
breath. Consequently, he had a tough time
concerning his energy and overall health
throughout the entire weekend.

Around 2:15 that Thursday on the 4th, Mark
came back around then looked into Stuart's office
before departing. Experience having been a good
teacher, Stuart opted to leave as well not long
afterward and noticed on his way out the door the
boxes that had been there earlier had suddenly

disappeared.

He has since begun searching air sample devices and he collected the HVAC vent from out of his office, carefully sealing it inside a plastic bag so that it can be tested for chemical residue. On a different note, it's become apparent to me his morale is suffering as he continues to question why his life has been ruined.

*

"Let's play the devil's advocate," I said, "by asking the most obvious question. If you're convinced they've been gassing you – to use your terminology – why have you stayed?"

"It's complicated," Stuart replied, "but there are a couple of reasons. For one, once you've been black-balled like I have - made to feel hungry and desperate - it's a place you don't ever want to end up again. They've paid me well, and as an independent contractor, I've more or less been able to write my own ticket while I've been there in that I come and go as I please without having to answer for each and every one of my movements. As long as I do my work, they more or less leave me alone … except for the chemicals that is.

"Also, I've informed them of my suspicions, and I've taken certain steps to protect myself," he continued.

"I get where you're coming from," I said in agreement. "What steps have you taken to protect yourself?" I asked.

"I've gotten a fan for my desk to help circulate the air in my office, and I've shut off the vent in there as well. I've also done my research, and I've put them on notice. Otherwise, once I'm hit with the sweet smell, I immediately exit the building while holding my breath, before they have a chance to hit me with the second chemical."

"I see," I replied while I continued furiously taking notes, "Anything else?" I asked.

"I guess you could say I've developed a heightened sense of awareness. Nothing gets past

me, so I don't take any unnecessary risks,"
Stuart concluded.

"And you think that's enough?" I asked.

"It has been so far, but I have to admit, I'm
getting tired of playing these games. I've
stopped going to meetings, because they gassed me
in the previous meeting. So I wasn't going to
show up and have it happen again. In fact, lately
I've been ready to walk out on my job several
times. I even called last Tuesday and told them I
wouldn't be back until Monday. At this point, I
just want to be left alone," he confided.

"And what was their response?" I asked.

"Not much of anything. They told me to take
care of myself and nothing more," Stuart said.

"Well then, why do you think they've kept you
on?" I asked, going off on a different tangent.

"I've thought about that," he responded, "I
think it goes back to *keeping your friends close
but your enemies closer,*" he replied. "This way
they can at least monitor me, while controlling
me with the chemicals."

"I understand," I replied sympathetically, "I don't know how you've taken it this long. What do you think you'd do if you left?" I asked.

"I don't know exactly. I guess I'm hoping this book will lead the way," Stuart concluded.

"I hope so," was all I said in return. By now I believed our missions had become one and the same. He needed peace, and I hoped my efforts could in some small way help to provide just that.

*

OFF THE RECORD: It should be noted that MedCollect is a totally owned subsidiary and thereby an extension of a much larger organization controlled by the Great Lakes Distributors of Little Rock who happen to monopolize alcohol distribution within the state of Arkansas. Since the days of prohibition, Arkansas – with the exception of a few small pockets within the state that include Little Rock, Hot Springs and the Northwest corner of the state where Fayetteville is located, has been more or less dry in terms of alcohol sales. However – despite its historically strong ties to the Bible belt - in recent years, there has been a well-orchestrated push to legalize alcohol sales statewide, which would favorably impact the Great Lakes Distributors to such a great extent it would be difficult to calculate in simple dollars and cents.

17 A FINAL APPEAL

I reached a point in Stuart's journal that concerned me. To me it spoke volumes about the fear his life might be in danger during the time in which he composed his plea to some as yet unknown source to come to he and his family's aid. Although it had been written some time ago, and by now appearances had led me to believe he was in a much more solid place psychologically, the fact he'd ever felt compelled to write such an plea acted as confirmation that those who sought to do him harm had in fact - on some level - accomplished their means, which made me more determined than ever to do all I could to help

see he got justice in this matter.

*

Exhibit L. Following is an excerpt taken

directly from his notes and serves as his appeal

for help:

To whom it may concern,

My wife, children and I have gone through many different situations and circumstances over the past seven years that would make our lives a good *20/20* or *60 Minutes* story. Maybe this letter will help to keep this from happening to someone else.

By writing these situations down and putting them in the order in which they have happened, it has been like reliving them all over again. This is a true story to the best of my knowledge. I have many notes over the past seven years to back up most situations. I hope that you will take this letter seriously and help me and my family to put an end to our persecution and suffering, and may justice be served.

There are at least 3 major situations that sometimes run parallel through this story. See if you can pick them out. In order to solve this story, an investigator, the IRS, maybe a lawyer, an accountant, a Real Estate Lawyer, and others will be needed. I am willing to give aid and help as much as possible. This story continues to grow as I remember things, but I will notify you as I remember of them.

I would like to express that I have tried to make sure everything is presented so you will understand what we have gone through and that we are not paranoid. This would be a great way of being able to discard the contents of this story. I will admit that having gone through all of this that I am very cautious and alert to things out of the ordinary. But I am not irrational.

Each time I have started over, something happened, although I was thinking that eventually I would be left alone. It is very hard to forgive and forget when the harassment hits you over and over.

You may ask why you have never come forward with this before. Well I have been threatened; I have been told they could set you up by running money through your bank account, and other negative words toward me. But why I am coming forward is, not until April of 2001 did I find evidence of money passing hands. And as my grandmother said when I told her what I had found, "God works in mysterious ways doesn't he."

So in closing, I pray that you will find the answers and restore to me what they have taken, and finally restore my name.

God be with you, and may justice be served,

Stuart Shockley 4/25/01

*

"In your notes, you stated in a letter titled *To Whom It May Concern:* that you had found evidence of money passing hands in April of 2001. Can you elaborate?" I asked.

"Sure, that refers to the real estate transaction I'd uncovered while at the courthouse between Paul Lancaster and his ex-wife back when Paul claimed to have been bankrupt. Remember, when I inquired she claimed to have been ripped off by Paul as a result of that transaction."

"Yes I recall," I replied before continuing,

"In addition, you also mentioned a conversation with your grandmother where she stated, 'God works in mysterious ways doesn't he?'. What was she referring to at the time?" I asked.

"That was when I told her about having accidentally found that same piece of evidence that was in direct contradiction to everything I had been told," Stuart replied.

"I see."

*

Still convinced he knew far more about what was going on than he'd revealed, it was at that same point Stuart began looking more closely into his father's activities. As such – in his own way – he began building a case against him.

*

"You've told me on several occasions that you believed your father got whatever settlement there was coming in your legal actions against

Paul Lancaster. Can you expound upon that?" I asked.

"Sure, as we discussed, my dad had beaten my wife and I to RJ Brown's office the following morning after the settlement hearing, long before we'd even had a chance to arrive, and then he gone without ever having spoken to me in relation to why he was there. We shared the same name. It would've been easy enough to transfer funds to an account bearing his name without provoking any questions. Besides, instinctively I knew he was aware of much more than he was sharing, and as a result I tried - with no success I might add - for 3-4 years to pry it out of him.

"Then just when I believed he was about to come clean, he died, somewhat mysteriously I might add," Stuart concluded.

"You said you did some checking into him, what did you uncover?" I asked.

"A duplicate Social Security Number for one,"

he confided. "When I checked into other possible SSN's for Robert S. Shockley, I discovered there was a duplicate under the name of Jerry E. Culver, and a death claim was filed for that social security number in April of 1988. The report then went on to state both my dad's and this Culver name was tied to my name, Robert S. Shockley, and my social security number as well."

"That's insane, had you ever heard the name Jerry E. Culver prior to that time?"

"Never," Stuart replied, "but I couldn't help thinking that's how they hid everything … under duplicate social security numbers."

*

"Your notes also mention an incident in which a state trooper tells you, 'I hope you get to keep this one,' referring to your *animal attracting invention*. Can you expand upon that?" I asked.

"Yeah that was when I wrecked my truck after

just having crossed the I-430 Bridge leaving Maumelle headed toward Little Rock. It was a driving rain and water was standing on the highway. You know how that hill winds upward at a steep grade. I'd just about made it to the top when I accidentally clipped one of those orange barrels. I flipped over, but I wasn't hurt.

"Anyway, this state trooper who wrote up the accident report said to me, 'I hope you get to keep this one,'" Stuart explained.

"In a town of several hundred thousand people, I don't know how he'd have known who I was much less what I'd been working on, but then everyone around me seemed to know more about what was going on than I did. After a while I guess you'd say it just became the new normal. It wasn't even the strangest conversation I'd ever had with a state trooper," he confided.

"What do you mean?" I asked.

"Well, once when Diana and I were attending

Toad Suck Days in Conway, we were standing in line to get a beer at *The Keg*. You know how slow those lines move, so we started talking to this guy standing there alongside us. While we were talking, another man comes up to the man we were talking to and asked him, 'Do you know who you're talking to?' and then left.

"We shrugged our shoulders and continued talking and this guy says, 'I appreciate what you're doing,', and then tells us he's a state trooper."

"How bizarre!" I commented.

"Anyway, months later I was reading in the newspaper something about an ordeal having to do with Clinton, and I saw this trooper named as one who had publicly come out against him, but I never knew exactly what he was referring to or even what became of him. For all I know he may be dead by now," Stuart concluded. As always, it made me feel like I was being used, but for what exactly I don't know."

*

OFF THE RECORD: Unfortunately, Stuart's father passed away under what can only be described as questionable circumstances prior to having answered any questions regarding Stuart's legal battles, thus leaving only Stuart's mother behind as a possible witness. However, if his mother is aware of anything out of the ordinary, she has not spoken a word, and any efforts toward getting her to open up have proven fruitless. Thus it would at least seem some secrets lie dead and buried in a grave bearing the marker Robert Shockley.

However – with that being said – there are still those who know far more than they've been willing to share at this point and they are alive and well. Among those names are Paul Lancaster and a host of attorneys beginning with Sam Strange and Steve Garver and ending with R.J.

Brown to name only a few of those who have either had direct contact or the opportunity to look into this case. Add to that same list all of Stuart's past employers and their associates, law enforcement, politicians and those who serve at their pleasure.

Why else would a former secret service agent – named Robert A. Fisak - whose card officially listed him as 'retired' have interrupted Stuart during an evening out this past year, directly insinuating himself between Stuart and his guest while having drinks at the Arlington Hotel? He then walked Stuart out to the steps leading up to the lobby entrance while explaining he used to be on the former first lady's detail (Hillary Clinton) while directly inquiring about Stuart's intentions.

While Hillary Clinton, herself, may not know Stuart's name, it's apparent someone within her close organization does and they have been instructed to keep an ever watchful eye on him.

However, when queried even Stuart hasn't a clue as to why he might have been approached aside from his speculations about her current presidential bid and a related effort to 'sweep the area' prior to the launch of her campaign.

Once this gentleman secured the information he wanted, he disappeared just as quickly as he'd arrived - stealth like - but he left his calling card behind, complete with contact numbers in both Atlanta and Palm Springs, Florida, and like so many bits and pieces of information, Stuart has held on to it since. It's hard not to be intrigued when you stare down at the embossed logo representing those who remain closest to the president and his family. These are the same individuals whose very oath of office declares they will protect and serve those whose lives they willingly place before their own.

*

The following three exhibits represent items

taken directly from Stuart's notes:

Exhibit M. represents specific inquiries Stuart made to his father prior to his death as it related to his ongoing suspicions that he was somehow involved behind the scenes.

For the past three to four year, I have discussed with you the situation concerning my family and all I have gone through as a result. I have also had people I've come into contact with point the finger to you. You have had a heart attack, and I would like for you to do whatever is necessary to end all hurt and wrong that has been done. I have given you chance after chance to come clean this is the last chance you will get.

A friend tells me there was 75000.00 dollars that was mine.

Some in Stocks.

Mom says she would like to "get her kitchen first" before I file suit against *Lavender & Wyatt*.

I cannot get a job.

Why did you say that I need to *get someone to trust me*, and then maybe they will tell me?

Who has ruined my name?

Where did you get the money to buy the land with Brian?

You do not work.

Mom does not work.

Exhibit N. represents Stuart's formal request for information concerning his own record with the FBI. His social security number has been removed for his own safety:

Robert Stuart Shockley

4 Northwood Dr.

Conway, AR 72032

Freedom of Information and Privacy Act Request

To: **FBI**

    1801 N Lamar #300

    Dallas, TX 75202

This letter constitutes my formal request for information pursuant to the provisions of the Freedom of Information and Privacy Acts, 5 USC 552.

I am requesting copies of all information maintained by your agency that pertain to me as described below:

Full Name: Robert Stuart Shockley

Current Address: 4 Northwood Drive, Conway, AR 72033

Social Security No.:   XXX-XX-XXXX

Date and Place of Birth: 10/15/57 Dallas, TX

Former Addresses: 1660 Blue Bird Lane, Conway, AR 72033

                          23 Lakeland Drive, Maumelle, AR

62 Broadmend, Drive, Little Rock, AR

64 Broadmend Drive, Little Rock, AR

Date:_____ Signature:_____

I, _____ a Notary Public in and for the county (city)
and state of _____ hereby certify that on the _____ day
of _____, 19__, before me personally appeared
_____, who is known by me to be the identical person
whose name is subscribed to, and who signed and executed the foregoing
instrument. In witness thereof, I have hereunto set my hand and official seal this
day and year above.

My commission expires:_____

Signature of Notary:_____

Exhibit O. represents the mysterious findings

associated with this search:

Possible Other Social Security Numbers Associated with Subject SHOCKLEY, ROBERT E ** ALERT ** SSN was issued to CULVER, JERRY, and a Death Claim for this ssn was filed in APR 1988. SHOCKLEY, ROBERT S SHOCKLEY, Possible Other Records/Names Associated with Social Security Numbers CULVER, JERRY E ** ALERT ** A Death Claim was filed in APR 1988.

Exhibit P. is a page taken directly from Stuart's

notes relating his and Diana's encounter with the

unnamed state trooper during *Toad Suck Days* in Conway, Arkansas:

Summer 97

While attending a street party in Conway. My wife and I went to the get a beer at the 'Keg.' While waiting in line we began to talk to a man. While talking another man came up and said to the man we were talking to "Do you know who your talking to?". Then he left. We continued talking and the man says, I appreciate what your doing?? He tells us he is a State trooper. Months later while reading the paper about the Clinton ordeal. I see the state troopers name in the paper as to one of the Troopers who was against Clinton.??? This makes me think that maybe that somebody is using me to

Exhibit Q. The following excerpt is the most complete online bio I was able to find concerning Mr. Robert A. Fisak. Although it states 23 years of service with the federal government, there is no mention of the Secret Service or Hillary Clinton.

---

*Background**

Mr. Robert A. Fisak served as Vice President of Operations of Undersea Recovery Corporation. Mr. Fisak founded and serves as president of a security consulting company providing business and legal support. He worked with Admiralty on its permitting activities and operational planning. Prior to his association with Admiralty, he served as an officer in a telecommunications company. Mr. Fisak was employed by the Federal Government for 23 years. He held various research and operational positions in the Treasury Department and at the Board of Governors of the Federal Reserve System. Prior to his Federal service, he was an Officer in the United States Army. Mr. Fisak served two tours in Vietnam and completed other assignments in the United States and Europe. He serves as a Member of Advisory Board of ID Watchdog, Inc. Mr. Fisak graduated from the University of Maryland with a BA in Economics, and continued his education with postgraduate studies at George Washington University.

"Undersea Recovery Group Corp (UNDR:OTC US)." *Executive Profile* Robert A. Fisak.* Bloomberg Business. Web.

Exhibit R. The following is a picture I snapped during a dinner meeting between Stuart Shockley and myself. It represents the card Robert A. Fisak left with Stuart the night he walked him out onto the steps facing the Arlington Hotel in Hot Springs. It was then he uttered the words, "Trust but verify …" to Stuart, which ultimately became the impetus behind the writing of this book.

18 IT HAS A NAME

A paranoid schizophrenic is someone who has figured out what's going on ….

Anonymous

One day Stuart called me during his trip home from work outside of Little Rock. While doing some searching online, he'd stumbled upon some terminology that was previously unknown to him that he wanted me to look into with regard to my ongoing research. When I asked what it was, he replied *gang stalking*.

*

The concept of gang stalking has actually been around for some time now. In the past, elite agencies such as the Secret Service were able to

expand and grow due to the existence of a
perceived threat to our much beloved freedom due
to communism and the fear of its spread to
democratized nations like the United States.
However, communism ceased to be a threat the day
the Berlin Wall fell back in 1990. Therefore the
world at large both seemingly and naturally
evolved into more of a peace-oriented community
devoted to the upholding of human rights while
keeping an ever watchful eye out for less obvious
threats of a covert nature.

It would then be logical to assume this fear
was somehow born out of the events which lead up
to the 9-11 attacks against the Twin Towers and
Pentagon – as well as the downed airliner in a
rural Pennsylvania field – that had once again
given birth to the kind of surreptitious behavior
condoned and conducted at the highest levels of
government – thus making it not only acceptable –
but also palatable in terms of keeping us safe.
However, that would require denying certain
evidence that such tactics were never really

disbanded to begin with following the collapse of communism.

Illegal projects like COINTELPRO – which stands for Counter Intelligence Program – and MK-ULTRA – a code name for a covert human research program - performed by United States organizations such as the FBI and CIA among others may have officially stopped, but gang stalking and electronic harassment are much more advanced, better versions of their predecessor. Therefore, it is more likely than not if you live in a NATO country the same happens in your nation each and every day. In fact, once the US government signed the Patriot Act into law back in 2001, a declaration of war was issued to all citizens of the world both great and small once they are in some way declared an enemy of the state. Names among those who have been known to have been targeted in the past include Dr. Martin Luther King, the American Indian Movement, and almost all groups protesting the Vietnam War.

Well known programs such as these began in

the 1950's and continued through the late 1960's. Published evidence indicates that programs such as MK-ULTRA *used many methodologies to manipulate individual mental states and alter brain functions* according to the STOPEG Foundation, which included *surreptitious administration of drugs and other chemicals, hypnosis, sensory deprivation, isolation, and verbal and sexual abuse.*

Gang stalking is also known as (state sponsored) organized stalking and is the method most used by a secret service to eliminate people. The reason why is because it's considered to be almost wholly obscure; however, as it applies to Stuart's case, it has been effectively used to steal his ideas, inventions and other intellectual property – which may seem far-fetched to some – but when you consider Edward Snowden's comments on December 17, 2013, *"These programs were never about terrorism: they're about economic spying, social control and diplomatic manipulation. They're about power …,"*

Stuart's continued harassment, which has endured over a period of nineteen plus years, becomes far more believable. This particular act of destroying an innocent person's life through the use of covert harassments, including systematic exposure to chemical toxins, constant feedback and innuendo as it directly related to personal events nobody but Stuart and his attorney could have possibly known at the time, as well as the questionable death of his father have all combined to almost ruin his mental state and his credibility, while keeping him close to his enemies at all times so that he may prove useful whenever the occasion presented itself.

*

According to dataasylum.com a targeted individual (TI) is the victim of this organized movement, which basically occurs in three stages:

1. The TI's movements are monitored at all times.

2. The TI's subsequent outrage leads to him becoming a publically harassed individual due to well-plotted, organized gang stalking.

3. The TI's body is randomly injured in some way to increase overall instability and confusion.

The same website further contends the class of people who design and fund such programs as this *run the world* … more accurately the governmental/money/commercial super trusts.

*

Within the course of my research, I've read over countless personal accounts attributed to gang stalking, and consequently I found myself questioning the validity of most taking into account mental illness and science's inability to reach certain people through the combined use of drugs and therapy. Another percentage could also be attributed to the so-call conspiracy theorists that have devoted much of their lives to uncovering certain hidden truths hidden behind legends like Area 51 and purported visits by aliens.

Many within the psychiatric community like to point to the internet when it comes to placing blame on the supposed escalated incidence of gang stalking type phenomenon taking place as is evidenced by the excerpt below:

Psychiatrists and psychologists have at least partially blamed the internet itself for such theories, citing an "extreme community" that encourages delusional thinking – that people in red and white cars are watching them, individuals lurking by their bedside as they sleep, and seemingly complete strangers are actually snickering at them in public the New York Times describes.

Although the internet has helped many afflicted with mental health problems, psychiatrists suggest a "dark side of social networking," where the mentally ill can have delusional theories reinforced.

"The views of these belief systems are like a shark that has to be constantly fed," Dr. Hoffman told The New York Times. "If you don't feed the delusion, sooner or later it will die out or diminish on its own accord. The key thing is that it needs to be repetitively reinforced."

Hoffman added that many of his research subjects have mentioned that they have visited mind-control sites that have confirmed their own paranoid suspicions.

"Gang-Stalking and Electronic Mind Control Community Spreads." *Atlanta.cbslocal.com,* 17 May 2014. Web.

*

While I tend to agree with Dr. Hoffman in that the internet does foster and breed a connected community amongst those living on the edge of reason who might otherwise have remained strangers, Stuart on the other hand only recently became aware of the incidence of gang stalking while performing an online search. Therefore, this same community couldn't have possibly fanned the flames of controversy and conspiracy over his last nineteen years, much less created the suspicion that something out of the ordinary was happening all around him. In addition, he has collected a mountain of evidence to support his claims.

*

There is at least an undeniable consistency throughout each thread that leads one to believe at least some of them are on to something. Even Hollywood has adopted this theme in a number of films including: *Control Factor (2003), The Informers (2008), The Adjustment Bureau (2011), Daddy, I'm a Zombie (2011), Earthkiller (also 2011) and Ultrasonic (2012).* In 2006's *A Scanner Darkly*, veteran actor Keanu Reeves' character states, *"Whatever it is that's watching … it's not human,"* referencing Nano-technology. While the movie industry is known for creating otherwise unimaginable images onscreen, they've also been instrumental when it comes to identifying trends that might go undetected long before their incidence becomes mainstream.

*

Another Hollywood connection is in direct relation the actress, Brittany Murphy, who died amidst dubious circumstances on December 20, 2009. Ms. Murphy had decided to testify in favor of a friend, Ms. Julia Davis, who at that time was whistle-blowing on the Department of Homeland Security for allowing terrorists to cross over the Mexican border due to lax security. There are those who believe she - Ms. Murphy - was killed due to the fact her celebrity status would have drawn unfavorable attention to these supposed government crimes.

Recently, her father had Ms. Murphy's hair samples released and tested by an independent lab who concluded she suffered from extremely toxic levels of at least 10 heavy metals found in her system. Many believe she and her husband were contaminated while in their residence and now both are deceased. Her husband, Simon Monjack, died five weeks following Ms. Murphy in the same house. While the Los Angeles County Coroner originally declared the actress' death was due to pneumonia, how likely is it that her husband would die of natural causes so soon afterwards?

While everyone must draw his or her own conclusions, I find it particularly interesting that both Ms. Murphy's supposed poisoning and Stuart's seemed to revolve around lawsuits, which lends credence to the various claims associated with the legal and or political nature of such attacks, as well as to the organized efforts required to achieve a desired goal. But why was Stuart still alive?

*

Interestingly enough, during my attempt to tie gang stalking directly to the kind of regular gasing Stuart had described at length, I came across an article entitled *250 Cases of Torture From Europe* where on page 186 a targeted individual described being poisoned in a strikingly similar manner, and I paraphrase … *it started to smell either sweetly or of an unknown chemical compound …"*

"250 Case Torture From Europe." *To You Our Selected Witnesses.* Docslide.us. Web.

*

And finally, in my quest to lend validity to this argument as a possible explanation for what's occurred over the past two decades in Stuart's life, I sought other credible support for such phenomenon. As such, I was able to find a rather impressive list of doctors who wholeheartedly believe in the existence of gang stalking. Following is a list of those individuals, as well as the web address that will take you to where you may read more:

Dr. Alfred Webre (Doctor of Jurisprudence in International Law) prepared a video appearance for the first Covert Harassment Conference in Brussels in 2014. The Wikipedia article about Alfred Webre became suddenly unnotable and fringe. It was deleted in May 2015. It had been online for 11 years. If it's unnotable fringe, then why does it take 11 years to realize that?

Dr. Anna Fubini (Doctor of Medicine) helps victims who suspect that they have implants.

Michael Segalov claims that he visited Assistant Professor Dr. Brian Sharpless (Ph. D. clinical psychology) because of exploding head syndrome. He claims that the doctor told him: "Gang stalking means that a group of people spies on you and makes your life as harsh as possible, and willingly makes you experience these hard explosions," and that he explained that some victims believe that they are being followed by some government agency. "They believe that this type of secret services uses a microwave generator, and that they point it at them at night and willingly cause the explosions." Brian Sharpless contact information. Brian Sharpless curriculum.

Dr. Corkin Cherubini (Ph. D. education) wrote on his website: *"I knew something was amiss, and afloat, when I kept seeing military type helicopters hovering over my home, and government vehicles everywhere — following, waiting, stalking in legions. I kept wondering, 'Could I have done something to make them think I might be a… terrorist, or whatever?' Then, I heard about 'The War on Whistleblowers,' but it would still be another four months before I heard of Government Gang Stalking!"* He runs 2 websites about gang stalking. www.paangelini.comwww.paangelini7.com

Dr. Gerald Sosbee (Doctor of Jurisprudence) believes that the Mafia is behind gang stalking. He's the most credible person who wrote about gang stalking. He's a lawyer, a former university instructor, a former FBI agent, a former police instructor, a former judge (Judge of City Court and Magistrate of the State of Texas), and a former private investigator. He believes that the purpose is that you become violent so you can be arrested or killed. www.SosbeeVFBI.com

Dr. Henning Witte (Doctor of Jurisprudence) interviews implant victims for the ICAACT website.

Dr. Jean Maria Arrigo (Ph. D. psychology, social psychologist and oral historian) wrote: *"In 'CIA no touch torture makes sense out of mind control allegations,' Cheryl Welsh provides a valuable overview of methods common to neuroweapons research and torture interrogation. Her essay is informed by the multitude of self-identified, experimental targets of neuroweapons researchers whom she represents. Scholars and journalists who are only able to track neuroweapons research and interrogation methods through government documents have biased the consensus reality in favor of government authorities who deceive the public. We owe thanks to Cheryl Welsh and her colleagues for their pioneering efforts to penetrate government deception through the phenomenology of self-identified victims of neuroweapons."*

Dr. John Hall (Doctor of Osteopathic Medicine) wrote 2 books about electronic harassment.

† Dr. Myron May (Doctor of Jurisprudence) tried to expose gang stalking and electronic harassment by shooting 3 people in a university library.

Dr. Nick Begich (Doctor of Naturopathic Medicine) addressed the European Parliament in 1998 about electronic harassment. He's the brother of Senator   Mark Begich, and the son of   Nicholas Begich, who posthumously won the 1972 election in Alaska.

† Dr. Rauni Kilde (Doctor of Medicine) spoke at the first Covert Harassment Conference in Brussels in 2014.

Dr. Reinhard Munzert (Doctor of Medicine) runs a website about electronic harassment.   www.MikrowellenTerror.de (*"microwave terror"* in English)

† Dr. Robert Becker (Doctor of Medicine) wrote in his book The body electric from 1985: *"Such a device has obvious applications in covert operations designed to drive a target crazy with 'voices' or deliver undetectable instructions to a programmed assassin."*

Dr. Scott Johnson (Ph. D. theology) was ordained in 1997 and later founded Freedom Family Fellowship, a non-denominational church located in Four Oaks, NC. He said: *"I had a lot of people who emailed me over the years about this, about they believe they have been electronically targeted with certain types of electronic warfare and mind control and I, you know, totally believe these people."* www.ContendingForTruth.com

Dr. Seth Farber (Ph. D. psychology) wrote: *"Directed energy weapons are among the high-tech arms of the century. They hurt and kill with electromagnetic power. Microwave weapons can be aimed at computers, electrical devices, and persons. They have strong physical and psychological effects and can be used for military and terrorist activities. These weapons are also part of crimes (in Europe) that almost nobody knows except the victims and the offenders. Until now they make the perfect crime possible. No doubt, these weapons have a terrible future."* www.SethHFarber.com

Dr. Terry Robertson (Doctor of Osteopathic Medicine) became an activist of FFCHS.

Dr. Tomo Shibata (Ph. D. sociology) blames the Mafia for gang stalking.

Dr. Vadim Baranov (Doctor of Medicine, oncologist) got asylum in the UK and the USA. www.BaranovFamily.org

"Doctors Who Believe in Gang Stalking." *Gang Stalking*. KIWIPEDIA The Honest Encyclopedia. Web.

*

"Let's get personal …" I said, leading

Stuart.

"What do you mean?" He asked, "It's all been personal."

"I'm referring to a specific incident of having been poisoned," I explained.

"Funny you should mention that," Stuart said as he sifted through a stack of papers, "I happen to come across something just yesterday that made me mad all over again. Remember, I called you about it, but I didn't want to go into it over the phone."

"I remember," was all I said while waiting to see exactly what he'd come up with during his search.

It was then he handed me a couple of papers, and I recognized the heading immediately. *Sorrells Research Lab and Field Services* had been a company my parents had been associated with for years, as they did the regular testing on our waste-water treatment plant behind my parent's shopping center outside of Hot Springs.

"What's this?" I asked, staring at the official report.

"It's the test results of a gray ash powder I collected all over my apartment in Little Rock after the maintenance people had been in earlier that day while I was out to work," Stuart explained.

"Let me backtrack a little bit … For a while, I moved to Westside Creek Apartments off Cantrell Road in Little Rock near the athletic center. My apartment was situated right next to the maintenance area. Twice they told me pest control had to enter my apartment to perform regular maintenance while I was away.

"The first time, when I returned home I couldn't help noticing this really fine gray powder piled up at my door and scattered in the carpet so I scooped some up and sealed it inside a jar so that I could have it tested. Those papers are the results of that test," Stuart confided.

I looked down at the words printed on the page, and of course they meant nothing to me. After all, I'm a writer not a chemist. So I asked

Stuart to bring up the internet, which he did and

then subsequently typed in the word

Acenaphthylene.

Acenaphthylene is a polycyclic aromatic hydrocarbon. The molecule resembles naphthalene with positions 1 and 8 connected by a C_2H_2 unit. It is a yellow solid. Unlike many polycyclic aromatic hydrocarbons, it has no fluorescence, as cited in Wikipedia.

The following website defines its uses and potential risks:

Acenaphthylene Synthesis

The compound is produced during combustion of natural fibers. It can be produced from 1-Acetoxyacenaphthene (C14H12O2) and 4-Amino-1,8-Naphthalimide (C12H8N2O2). It is a common ingredient in coal tar and crude oil. It is also often produced as an industrial or municipal waste. Coal tar distillation is another way of producing this substance.

Acenaphthylene MSDS

The chemical is commonly released in the environment by disposal of factory and industrial sewage and waste byproducts. This substance is also produced by coal tar distillation.

Humans are generally infected by this compound by inhalation or dermal contact where the content of this chemical is high. The chemical exists as vapor in the air. Drinking water supplies can also get contaminated by this chemical and prove to be a health hazard for humans. People swimming or taking baths in water contaminated with this chemical can also get infected. This can lead to health disorders such as skin cancer.

Acenaphthylene Toxicology

Toxicology data on this substance shows that it is harmful to health if it is swallowed or inhaled or absorbed by skin. Exposure to the eyes or the respiratory organs can cause subsequent irritation and health damage. A person might suffer from lung cancer if his or her respiratory organs are exposed to this chemical.

The compound goes through biodegradation in the surrounding environment.

Critical Areas of Acenaphthylene Infection

The areas that are most vulnerable to infection include

- Lungs
- Skin
- Eyes
- Nervous system
- Mucous membranes

"Acenaphthylene." Chemistry Learner. Web.

*

Then I asked Stuart to look up the second compound listed, namely octachloro and the word printed at the top of the second page, Semi-Volatiles …. A quick search on Yahoo provided an answer:

Octachloro Dipropylether | molecular formula: C6H6CL8O CAS#: 127-90-2 , Synonyms: Octachloro-dipropyl ether;2,3,3,3,2',3',3',3'-Octachlorodipr... Ether; Coils containing pyrethroid insecticides, particularly d-allethrin, may contain octachlorodipropyl ether (S-2, S-421) as a synergist or active ingredient.

Two studies published in Environmental Health Perspectives indicates that mosquito coils with octachlorodipropyl ether (S-2) are effective but release high levels of carcinogens. The coils, unregistered in the US, are used in southeast Asia. See the papers Mosquito Coil Emissions and Health Implications and Octachlorodipropyl Ether (S-2) Mosquito Coils Are Inadequately Studied for Residential Use in Asia and Illegal in the United States....

Semi-Volatile Organic Compounds

This Fact Sheet is presented by the U. S. Environmental Protection Agency, Region III (EPA) to assist in the selection of analytical parameters and the associated Quality Assurance and Quality Control (QA/QC) procedures to be utilized in Phase II Environmental Assessments under the U.S. Environmental Protection Agency (EPA) Brownfields initiative. This fact sheet is presented for informational purposes only, and should not be construed as a federal policy or directive. The Brownfields Coordinator for this region may be reached at 215-814-5000.

A semivolatile organic compound is an organic compound which has a boiling point higher than water and which may vaporize when exposed to temperatures above room temperature. Semivolatile organic compounds include phenols and polynuclear aromatic hydrocarbons (PAH).

*

After looking over the information regarding the chemicals detected, I could see no reason why they should have been used in someone - anyone's - apartment. Sure these were chemicals detectable in certain pesticides, but this particular compound had been banned in the United

States and in no way should have been used to exterminate the interior of one's living space considering their use came with stern warnings about the necessity of avoiding exposure due to serious potential health hazards.

"What did you do when you got the test results?" I asked.

"Wait, that's not all," Stuart interrupted prior to answering my question.

"What do you mean that's not all?" I replied.

"When I was informed they were coming in a second time, I rigged up a recording device. Unfortunately, video wasn't really available back then, so I could only record voices," he explained.

"What did you hear?" I asked.

"The only thing I could hear of significance was, 'I wonder where he keeps it …' but they never said what they might be looking for," Stuart confided.

"Do you have any thoughts about that?" I

queried.

"It could have been anything I suppose. It's been so long ago I'd actually forgotten about the incident until I ran into these papers, but it was clear they weren't there to look at the water heater as I'd been told," he concluded.

"So how did you handle the intrusion?" I asked once more.

"I sent them a letter, but nothing was resolved, so I wound up leaving. The letter's pretty much self-explanatory," Stuart suggested. I took it in hand and began reading its contents.

After I finished my reading, I had little to contribute except for the following … "In essence, I suppose you did what you had to do to survive by removing yourself from an intolerable situation."

*

OFF THE RECORD: I find it's far easier to dismiss the probability of gang stalking versus believing it exists. To those of us seemingly sane individuals who go through life rather unscathed, we tend to want to isolate ourselves from what appears just a little bit crazy or outlandish on the surface, while preferring instead to keep moving through life with blinders on the same way a thoroughbred race horse who doesn't wish to confront his opponents strides around the racetrack. But what works in sport doesn't always translate well in real life, especially when you're the one whose life is being ruined. Therefore, it might be more prudent and wise to at least accept gang stalking as a viable possibility while hoping it never actually happens to you.

Although initially having been so excited about coming across gang stalking, after reading through several websites, Stuart told me himself he didn't wish to be associated with this group, as he perceived it 'too far out there' and believed it had no merit in his case. I – on the other hand – preferred to do my own clinical research, which at best was a little more objective seeing as I had not been one of its *victims.*

Thus after reading through a considerable amount of evidence and claims, I thought it best to include this chapter as a possible explanation of how one highly organized, behind-the-scenes effort could seek to systematically dismantle a man's life to the point he remains so distracted just trying to survive that he's virtually unable to pursue the real matters at hand, that being the enforcement of his patent and protection of his intellectual property. Therefore, while he remained otherwise occupied, others were exploiting his genius thereby feathering their own nests while making millions – if not billions – in the process, thereby leading me to believe Stuart Shockley is indeed the 'targeted individual' at the center of a campaign other high-level and far more informed individuals might refer to as 'gang stalking'.

*

Exhibit S. This is the official lab report Sorrells provided on the powdery substance Stuart collected from out of his apartment. There are two pages.

Exhibit T. Shows the letter Stuart composed and forwarded to the management of Westside Creek Apartments in Little Rock citing the chemical contamination.

SORRELLS RESEARCH
LABORATORY AND FIELD SERVICES

WEF

8002 Stanton Road
Little Rock, Arkansas 72209

CHEMISTS
ECOLOGISTS
CONSULTANTS
PLANNERS

Phone 501-562-8139
Fax 501-562-7025
Toll Free 1-800-331-8139

LABORATORY ANALYSIS

```
                            Date of Report: February 26, 2004
                            Date Received : February  9, 2004

        For: SHOCKLEY, S
             APT#1146
        Job: GC/MS SCAN.
Sample From: APT# 1146 / WSC


ANALYTE                                  RESULT UNITS      METHOD
----------------------------------- - ------------- ---------- ------

Acenaphthylene, octachloro-             =    1.000 Present     625
```

```
STANDARD METHODS, 18TH ED.; EPA METHODS, 3RD ED.
Collected by:
S. SHOCKLEY  on 02/09/04 at 11:45
Analysis by :
SEE ATTACHED QUALITY ASSURANCE PAGE.
        Sample preservation and Laboratory Analysis conducted according to EPA
40 CFR Part 136. Test/Analyst/Time/Coeff./Var./ QA plan filed with ADPC&E.
Includes 10 % replication and 10 % recovery studies by random selection.
Instruments maintained and calibrated and records kept.
See Attached.

        Copies to:
   MR. S, SHOCKLEY



Laboratory Number: 4050.001    BJB Reviewed By: K. E. Sorrells, M.S. [
```

**SORRELLS RESEARCH
LABORATORY AND FIELD SERVICES**

8002 Stanton Road
Little Rock, Arkansas 72209

CHEMISTS
ECOLOGISTS
CONSULTANTS
PLANNERS

Phone 501-562-8139
Fax 501-562-7025
Toll Free 1-800-331-8139

QUALITY ASSURANCE

February 9, 2004
The following QA represents SRA's Quality Assurance values for this report.

ANALYTE	ANALYST	BEG. DATE	BEG. TIME	FIN. DATE	FIN. TIME	S.D. %	SPK. REC.	#IN BAT
Semi-Volatiles (Surr. Avg	CAS	02/12/04	1214	02/12/04	1247	3.74	113.8	1

Field PH/TEMP/D.O. Sampler or Courier/ at time of sampling or pick up
Sample preservation and laboratory analysis conducted according to EPA
40 CFR Part 136   TEST/ANALYST/TIME/COEF. VAR.* QA PLAN filed with
ADPC&E. Include replication.

KES = K. E. Sorrells
JBS = James B. Sorrells
CAS = Cecil A. Sorrells
MKM = Mark Kyle McKenzie

KESII = K. E. Sorrells, II
TJS = Todd J. Sanders
JHD = J. Henry Dodson

Laboratory Number: 4050.001   BJB

03/08/04

WestSide Creek Apartments

Management,

Since the second entry into my apartment by the Pest Control people I have had continuance burning sensations to my eyes, nose, throat and respiratory system . Some of the poison used was piled up 1 1/2 inches along the wall of my apartment and in the breezeway as well as in the door entry way to my apartment.

These health problems not as severe as they were continue to persist each time I stay in my apartment. Which I have only stayed there 14 out of the last 28 days.

I also took a sample of the poison and had it tested. A copy is attached showing the chemical analysis of the test. Along with data sheets and information on the chemicals.

So far I have stayed in a motel room $55.00. Spent $190.00 on chemical analysis test. I have to sleep with the windows open and use an air purifying system to stay in my apartment but still continue to have the symptoms I mentioned above.

When I stay away from my apartment this symptoms go away.

Please take me serious and lets talk about what can be done so that I can enjoying living in my apartment.

Stuart Shockley   Apartment #1146 WestSide Creek Apartments

Exhibit U. Is an excerpt from the log Stuart maintained during the period of time he was employed by Bartman Systems. It details certain questionable events as they occurred in real time relating to potential gang stalking incidents:

NOTES OF EVENTS

FOR ABOUT THE 3rd or 4th time in 2 years. on April 2,3, 1998 the phone wouldn't work. The phone Company came out and within 30 minutes & had had it fixed in thirty minutes.

> FRIDAY MAR 16, 1918, THE PAINTE OUT
> WORKING AROUND 3:00 PM. THE PHONE CO
> SAID THEY COULD NOT BE HERE TIL THE
> 11 of MARCH

> SUNDAY or of MAR, THE Phone is working when we come
> home, The Phone Co had left a message saying
> that the line is good up to our house.

The above references illustrate how much
difficulty Stuart and his wife are having with
regard to maintaining a working telephone line.

> END APRIL, They (candy &?) said that if you go
> to California. They will give a 75,000
> bonus, 75,000 a year, to 100,000 after 2 years.
> This shows they want me out of the state.

The above excerpt outlines an exchange that took
place between an employee at Moss's Equipment –
one of the companies Stuart was contracted out to
during his tenure with Bartman Systems – and
himself.

It's Stuart's contention someone wanted him out
of Arkansas during that time and as such was

willing to dangle a pretty big carrot as an incentive. He further contends Cindy S. was being used as a pawn to deliver a message designed to test the waters.

A rather ominous notation above is in direct relation to an incident where Stuart was exposed to harmful gases and his subsequent reaction, which led to his calling the FBI. During questioning, the interviewer seemed to take a particular interest in Daymark, yet another company Stuart had been contracted out to during this same time and the one tasked with the delivery of all of Walmart's frozen foods. He even went so far as to suggest Stuart relocate,

as was alluded to in his comment about gang-

related violence and 'drive-bys'.

Another Daymark incident, this one serves as

evidence he was being exposed to toxic fumes with

regard to his mention of light-headedness and

sudden loss of coordination, in addition to loss

of memory. He does his best to note not only the

date, but exact date and time of incident.

> Mon Nov 8 - Working at Firestone in Russellville around noon a smell in the air carried from on Nov 4. On Nov 12 at noon at Marrville office a smell was present (chemical smell). I got sick at my stomach, headache, nausea.

Above represents two additional examples of
exposure after having been sent to a remote
location by Bartman's, his employer at that time.

> Nov 16, 98 Went to Axiom for interview. Put door check on door. Came out to leave after interview door check was out of back door. ???

> June 23, TUES I put CHECK SETTINGS ON MY CAR DOORS ONE HAD BEEN RELEASED & COULD NOT BE FOUND ON THE DRIVER DOOR. WHEN I WENT TO LUNCH. THIS MEANS THE DOOR HAD BEEN OPEN.
> 24 BACK DOOR WAS UNTRIGGERED
> 25 AT MY HOUSE BACK DOOR UNTRIGGERED.

At one point, Stuart began setting 'checks' in
his car doors and trunk as well as his home by
wedging something small and not easily detectable
with a mere glance in between the actual door and
its frame. This way he could tell if the door had

been opened by someone in his absence. The above entries reference two separate occasions in which those same checks had been disturbed.

19 THE BILDERBERG GROUP

Throughout history there have been numerous rumors of so-called secret societies whose elite membership practiced highly confidential rituals behind sealed doors while plotting courses of action known only to them, thus leaving those of us on the outside the ability to only speculate about their power and what methods they chose to yield such power in order to forward their surreptitious ambitions. One of these secret societies has only recently been brought to my attention; however, before I elaborate, I'd like to offer up a brief review of the top ten as outlined in much greater detail on *Listverse.com*.

*

Established in 1832, the famed *Order of the Skull and Bones* – formerly known as the *Brotherhood of Death* – is the oldest student secret society in the United States whose membership boasts former presidents, George H.W. Bush and son, George W. Bush. Even today they still meet on campus in a building referred to as the 'Tomb' on Thursdays and Sundays each week, and it has often been rumored the organization has been the incubator for the CIA despite the agency's continued protests to that effect.

Perhaps more commonly recognized however, would be the *Free Masons*, and/or the *Scottish Rite* whose often extravagant meeting halls and equally elaborate rituals are associated with architecture, as evidenced by the compass and square symbols associated with the group. Membership is by invitation only – through an existing member – and those accepted must complete specific rituals to ascend to the highest order of degrees. There are specific use of multiple signs and handshakes to gain admission to meetings, as well as to identify possible other members of the organization who support each other in any and all endeavors.

While they refer to God as the Great Architect of the Universe, most churches strictly frown upon membership, particularly the Roman Catholic Church, whereupon the act of practicing Free Masonry comes with the possible punishment of excommunication. While I may very well be wrong in my assumption, I contend they are much more concerned with the architecture of society as opposed to the constructs of the universe.

Other lesser known groups – at least in modern terms – include the *Rosicrucians*, originally formed by German Protestants in the 1600's, the *OTO* or Order of the *Temples of the East* – who under Aleister Crowley's leadership – took on the principles of a religious system known as Thelema and is based around a single law, 'Do what thou wilt shall be the whole law, love is the law, love under the will,' (1904).

Moreover, the *Order of the Golden Dawn* is widely considered to be the forerunner of OTO and is largely taken from Christian mysticism, Qabalah, Hermeticism, the religion of Ancient Egypt, Freemasonry, Alchemy, Theosophy, magic and Renaissance writings. William Yeats and Aleister Crowley are two of the more famous members attributed to this group.

The *Knights Templar* is a modern offshoot of freemasonry and is *not* associated with the legends surrounding the original *Knights Templar* - a religious military group formed during the 12th century - and rumored to have been protectors of the Arc of the Covenant and King Solomon's treasures. Though they do not claim a direct tie to the medieval group, they do however suggest a *barrowing of both ideas and symbols.*

Then there are the *Illuminati* - now made famous by author Dan Brown in his book by the name of "Angels and Demons". Historically, they have been known as a movement of radicalized freethinkers whose focus remains on humanism and atheism. Born an offshoot of The Enlightenment, it was once thought this group all but collapsed during the late 1700's due to internal panic and dissention over the succession of a new leader. However, some believe a small faction did survive and that the *Skull and Bones* is actually an American version of the *Illuminati*, while still others maintain the *Illuminati* are still operating and managing the main actions of the governments of the world.

Then there is the group for which I maintain the most interest in terms of my work and how it applies to the topics at hand … *The Bilderberg Group*. Its name was originally taken from the location of the first meeting back in 1954 at the Hotel Bilderberg in the Netherlands.

It is less commonly known as a group of highly influential people who meet in secrecy every year under the protection of government and military sponsored security, and the topics discussed are kept top secret by those in attendance. Attendees pledge not to divulge topics of discussion, auspiciously under the guise that those present could not otherwise speak as freely should the fear that every spoken word be subsequently dissected and analyzed by mainstream media's 24-hour coverage. Consequently, controversy and conspiracies associated with this group continue to abound.

Before I go on to discuss my particular interest in *The Bilderberg Group*, there are two remaining organizations worth mentioning, each of which were made famous in Dan Brown's phenomenal best seller and movie by the same name "The Da Vinci Code". Both the *Priory of Scion* and the *Opus Dei* are supposedly centered on the protection of what they each individually esteem to be most sacred in all of creation, with the former as it relates to the purported actual blood decedents of Jesus and Mary Magdalene, whereas the latter is more concerned with the fortification of the Holy Roman Catholic Church. While some believe the Priory to be a fictional group who possess no historical significance, others maintain the mindset of *not so fast*.

Frater, Jamie. "Top Ten Secret Societies." *Listverse.com*. 27 Aug. 2007. Web.

*

Stuart had never heard of the *Bilderberg Group* until an opportune meeting that took place between him, his father and his uncle – his mother's brother – in a small town called Bald Knob that is situated about an hour northeast of Little Rock, Arkansas. At his wits end due to the ongoing surveillance and the subliminal torture he'd been experiencing at that time, there was a moment when Stuart gathered all his evidence and took it to his father house in order to seek his advice as to what he should do. During that exchange, Robert Shockley immediately suggested they have his Uncle Darrell take a look at it.

*

Darrell Throckmorton had always been something of an enigma in Stuart's family. Like so many southern kin, the Shockley-Throckmorton clans were ones who exhibited a kind of *feast or famine* mentality, meaning they were either very successful in their endeavors or not at all. Stuart's Uncle Darrell rated among the most affluent in the family, as exhibited by the fact he was well-respected and a member of high standing in the country club circuit and about town. Thus he was well known and catered to wherever he went.

When I asked Stuart what his uncle did for a living, he wasn't really certain, which is equally enigmatic considering Bald Knob's only claim to fame was that it was once a railway stop and had never developed into much of anything more. However, the logical assumption would be he was somehow associated with agriculture, which accounts for most of eastern Arkansas's acres upon acres of fields and pastures. When I tried to do an online search on his name, the only remarkable thing I was able to pull up was he was once the beneficiary of governmental farm subsidy which amounted to just over $1200, which further supported the agricultural assumption.

However, at that time Stuart's dad seemed convinced Darrell Throckmorton would have the answer he was seeking and was insistent they take all of Stuart's evidence to him. While there, Stuart's uncle took a close inspection of everything presented and then asked Stuart, "Have you ever heard of the *Bilderberg Group*?" And although he failed to elaborate on the inner-workings of the group itself, he seemed to have a full accounting of its current membership and their movements.

When I asked Stuart what his uncle's recommendations were, he said, "He told me I might be a little paranoid," which may or may not have been true. However, once again the exercise had proven to be yet another seemingly futile exercise wherein so few words were spoken, although there seemed to be a world of implications behind them, yet again leaving one who was totally inexperienced when it came to world politics with no clear answers or direction in which to turn.

*

A rather colorful and illustrious genealogical history of the Throckmorton name can be traced back to a famed English estate by the name of Coughton Court acquired through marriage back in 1409 and then subsequently rebuilt by Sir George Throckmorton, who dedicated its great gatehouse to King Henry VIII. Sir George was once favored by the infamous king right up until his divorce from first wife, Catherine of Aragon, who was a devout Roman Catholic and supporter of the mother church. Throckmorton - a staunch supporter of Catholicism himself - became notorious for having favored the Queen over the King in his efforts to end his marriage to Catherine, thus pitting him against the Reformation.

The name is also associated with the Throckmorton Plot of 1583 which sought to murder Queen Elizabeth I of England in favor of her Catholic cousin, Mary Queen of Scots, who was being held under house arrest at Loch Leven Castle during that time. After keeping her hostage in a number of different interior English locations, after eighteen and a half years Mary was eventually convicted of treason in the attempted murder of Queen Elizabeth and subsequently executed.

However, this was not the first brush the Throckmortons had with the historical Queen Elizabeth. Sir Walter Raleigh, famed writer, poet, politician and explorer – to name only a few of his accomplishments – once secretly wed Elizabeth Throckmorton, one of the Queen's Ladies in Waiting back in 1591 without the Queen's prior consent. Thus both Raleigh and his new bride were both subsequently incarcerated in the Tower of London.

Following his eventual release, Sir Walter Raleigh went on several notable expeditions of discovery to South America, which he chronicled in an exaggerated tale titled "El Dorado" but then went on to be arrested and executed in 1618, which was nothing more than a political move designated to appease the Spanish. Thought to have been one of the most notable figures of the Elizabethan Era, Sir Walter Raleigh was once featured as one of the 100 Most Notable Britons in a BBC poll back in 2002, according to Wikipedia.

*

Back to the Bilderberg Group … according to *The Independent*, in an article published online on August 20, 2015, amid all the speculation, there are at least four things we know for certain, first being where the meetings are held. In 2014 the annual gathering was held in the Danish capital, Copenhagen, and in 2015 the event was hosted at the Interalpen-Hotel Tyrol in the Austrian Alps with the 2016 location not readily available.

Stone, Jon. "4 Things We Know about the Secretive Bilderberg Group and 1 Thing We'll Never Know." *Independent.co.uk*. Independent, 9 June 2015. Web.

*

Second, the group does release a list of attendees ranging from top politicians to corporate giants, as well as a list of newcomers whose specific knowledge on certain topics of interest might prove valuable in terms of discussion. Among the familiar list of names both past and present are *David Rockefeller, Henry Kissinger, Bill Clinton, Gordon Brown, Angela Merkel, Alan Greenspan, Ben Bernanke, Larry Summers, Tim Geithner, Lloyd Blankfein, George Soros, Donald Rumsfeld, Rupert Murdoch, other heads of state, influential senators, congressmen and parliamentarians, Pentagon and NATO brass, members of European royalty, selected media figures, and invited others – some quietly by some accounts like Barack Obama and many of his top officials* according to *Global Research*.

Lendman, Stephen. "The True Story of the Bilderberg Group" and What They May Be Planning Now, A Review of Daniel Estulin's Book." *Globalresearch.ca.* Global Research, 25 May 2014. Web.

*

The same article profiles Daniel Estulin who wrote "The True Story of The Bilderberg

Group" originally published back in 2005 and then revised for a second publication in 2009. His alleged true story outlines the author's 14 year investigation into the elusive group's *aristocracy of purpose* between Europe and the United States dedicated to a *shadow world government*. Estulin goes on to contend *no one buys their way in*, as membership has an exclusive purpose aligned to their specific worldwide agenda.

Prior to each year's annual meeting, the group also publishes an itinerary covering a range of broad subject areas as outlined in the following list from 2015:

- Artificial Intelligence
- Cybersecurity
- Chemical Weapons
- Threats
- Current Economic Issues
- European Strategy
- Globalization
- Greece
- Iran
- Middle East
- NATO

- Russia
- Terrorism
- United Kingdom
- USA
- US Elections
  And finally, we also know security is

provided by the host

Country - who cooperates fully - and therefore provides police protection. Under no circumstances is private security, body guards, assistants or legal and personal attaches allowed, not to mention girlfriends, wives or husbands of the attendees. In addition, there is extensive security checks performed on any and all vehicles both entering and exiting the area and previous arrests have included a list of journalists attempting to gain confidential information from an attendee.

Estulin goes on to write:

Slowly, one by one, I have penetrated the layers of secrecy surrounding the Bilderberg Group, but I could not have done this without help of 'conscientious objectors' from inside, as well as outside, the Group's membership." As a result, he keeps their names confidential.

Whatever its early mission, the Group is now "a shadow world government….threaten(ing) to take away our right to direct our own destinies (by creating) a disturbing reality" very much harming the public's welfare. In short, Bilderbergers want to supplant individual nation-state sovereignty with an all-powerful global government, corporate controlled, and check-mated by militarized enforcement.

"Imagine a private club where presidents, prime ministers, international bankers and generals rub shoulders, where gracious royal chaperones ensure everyone gets along, and where the people running the wars, markets, and Europe (and America) say what they never dare say in public.

Furthermore, Estulin goes on to state Bilderberg

objectives include:

The Group's grand design is for "a One World Government (World Company) with a single, global marketplace, policed by one world army, and financially regulated by one 'World (Central) Bank' using one global currency." Their "wish list" includes:

- "one international identify (observing) one set of universal values;"

- centralized control of world populations by "mind control;" in other words, controlling world public opinion;

- a New World Order with no middle class, only "rulers and servants (serfs)," and, of course, no democracy;

– *"a zero-growth society" without prosperity or progress, only greater wealth and power for the rulers;*

– *manufactured crises and perpetual wars;*

– *absolute control of education to program the public mind and train those chosen for various roles;*

– *"centralized control of all foreign and domestic policies;" one size fits all globally;*

– *using the UN as a de facto world government imposing a UN tax on "world citizens;"*

– *expanding NAFTA and WTO globally;*

– *making NATO a world military;*

– *imposing a universal legal system; and*

– *a global "welfare state where obedient slaves will be rewarded and non-conformists targeted for extermination."*

*

It is at least somewhat widely accepted that Barack Obama and Hillary Clinton met with the exclusive group in secret somewhere in Northern Virginia back in 2008 while the press had boarded a plane headed back to Washington with the understanding the President was in route there himself. It has been speculated at that time the group gave its blessing to the impending Obama presidency in terms of meeting their immediate concerns with a future endorsement going to Hillary for 2016.

In an article written by Steve Watson, a London-based writer and editor for *Alex Jones' Infowars.com*, Watson contends *Hillary has a deep rooted connection to the Bilderberg elitists.*

Her husband Bill Clinton attended the 1991 meeting in Germany shortly before becoming President and he attended again in 1999 when the conference was held in Sintra, Portugal (despite Clinton's lie that he had not attended in 15 years).

Hillary herself was <u>*rumored to have attended*</u> *the 2006 meeting in Ottawa, Canada.*

Watson, Steve. "BILDERBERG BACKS HILLARY FOR 2016 PRESIDENCY Chief Hillary Advisor to Attend Secret Confab." *ALEX JONES' INFOWARS.COM BECAUSE THERE IS A WAR ON FOR YOUR MIND*. Infowars.com, 8 June 2015. Web.

*

OFF THE RECORD: While we may never know what Darrell Throckmorton's real occupation concerns happen to be or why he would possess intimate knowledge of a group whose membership demands the highest level of secrecy attached to such an elite organization, we can at least connect the dots between Arkansas, the Clintons political ambitions and the Bilderberg Group. However, what we will never know is why Stuart's father insisted he show all of his confidential records and notes to his uncle and why his uncle in turn asked Stuart if he'd ever heard of the Bilderberg Group, because one of those present is now deceased, one isn't talking and the other hasn't a clue.

My own speculation is that Robert Shockley wanted to accomplish two things … to show he was cooperating with the powers that be - the same people who were orchestrating the events surrounding his son's life - by revealing pertinent information, while at the same time appealing to his brother-in-law for protection for his son. If so, one might make the case he accomplished his mission.

However, if Stuart is correct in assuming that Robert A. Fisak's orchestrated second meeting between the pair of men at a barbeque restaurant in North Little Rock in which Mr. Fisak secured requested information in the form of a memory stick from Stuart (which did not include the whole story or relevant password information) had something to do with Hillary Clinton's intention to run for the presidency, then the Arkansas connection to the group becomes far more relevant indeed, particularly since Mr. Fisak was apparently offering Stuart 'something' in return.

Once again – while speaking in code – Mr. Fisak told Stuart he wanted him to 'put him up' or 'take care of him' whenever he came to town, despite the rather obvious observation Fisak had the means to secure his own accommodations.

When Stuart replied by telling Fisak 'he had no money' he recalled Fisak seemed instantly irritated by his seeming lack of cooperation.

However, on the very next evening following that luncheon while Stuart was having his usual cocktail while sitting at the Arlington Hotel's bar in downtown Hot Springs, a woman who he'd never seen before approached him and told him the building he'd always wanted directly across the street could be purchased in a private sale the following day and she left him with a number, instructing him to call. But once again he refused their offer, contending all he has ever wanted was to be paid fair market value for his intellectual property and then be left to live his life in peace.

20 THE FIVE SENSES

What is the relevance between the law as it pertains to legal precedence and our five senses? A good question, this very concept was once the center of focus at a *non-conference* held at the University of Westminster in London back in 2013. After which an attendee named Cedric Gilson, also a visiting fellow in law, composed a blog entitled, *Law and The Senses: Symposium, Performance, Phenomenon?* which was published online on June 25, 2013.

Following is a direct quote:

> *What is Law's relationship to senses? In a sense, Law, the anesthetic par*

excellence, is constantly engaged in numbing the sense into common sense; manipulating, channeling and controlling the sensible; inserting properties and forbidding contacts; dissimulating violence, regulating sounds and defining taste. However, senses are not static. Rather, they are shifting and elusive qualities, constantly reshuffled by socio-cultural and technological changes, always dislocating Law's normativity towards new potentialities. In this other sense, Law emerges from the senses, and whereas senses are a constant arena of legal machinations, they are also Law's constant blind spot and inescapable excess. Is there then a legal sensing, an illegal sensing, or even perhaps a sensing beyond the Law? How does Law sense? Can Law hear, taste, smell, touch, see? Can Law indulge in sensual pleasures, or is it confined to the anesthetic arena of common sense? Can senses be a tool to use, know and study Law better? Would this make Law more 'sensible', or instead more suffocating?

Gilson, Cedric. "Law and the Senses: Symposium, Performance, Phenomenome?" *Critical Legal Thinking – Law & the Political -*. Criticallegalthinking.com, 25 June 2013. Web.

*

In terms of the theft of Stuart Shockley's intellectual property and his subsequent manipulation and torment at the hands of so many others both in front of and behind the scenes, one must effectively 'drink the Kool-aide' made up of so-called logic in order to dull the senses and blur vision just enough to transform a fallacious set of circumstances that have occurred over the course of two decades into simple common sense.

But what if a new kind of law emerged – the result of having engaged our sight, sound, smell, taste and touch as combined with a healthy dose of cognition for the purpose of interpretation? Might we at least have a greater understanding of how the laws should apply to those who abuse their power against a seemingly defenseless individual who was simply trying to do his job?

It is Gilson's contention that while one cannot experiment with the law one can and should experiment with the application of the law so that the victim does not have to be condemned to a prison built by injustice due to the perpetuation of greed and a never-ending thirst for power. In terms of the potential juror, senses could be stimulated to achieve a greater capacity to respond to such cases that involve personal injury and civil disobedience exercised in reverse.

Far too many people distrust the government these days - and maybe with good reason - as Washington is perceived as being dysfunctional, while fewer and fewer registered voters are finding it difficult to make the case that their vote has the potential to make a difference. On those rare occasions when a visionary does come along running on a platform of change, he or she is often met with such resistance, social media lights up with literally millions of comments drawing parallels to the anti-Christ and the dreaded *end of days*.

In the face of such resistance, it would at least seem the concept of engaging the use of one's personal and individual consciousness might actually prove beneficial when it came to scoring one for the good guys … at least one who was intent on *making the world a better place* while refusing to sign onto the side of corruption. Then once again we might all have reason to cheer while watching the great Goliath fall victim yet again while the underdog rises up victorious, thereby restoring one's faith in the common good and the laws of the land. Then Arkansas – and America by extension – might once again become known as the *Land of Opportunity*.

*

In the United States – even within the throes of such widespread ambivalence - I think it's still fair to say most of us still hold fast to certain expectations … get an education, work hard, play fair and the potential for rewards are great, though certainly not guaranteed. We all seem to live somewhere on a sliding scale according to the dictates imposed by the socio-economic structure of wherever we happen to reside on that scale at any given moment in time. Therefore, the more prestigious school ultimately yields to a better education, which leads to a higher paying position and so forth.

However, on rare occasions, somebody intuitive, one who possesses a certain creative edge happens to do or design something so outstanding, it makes us all stand up and take notice. Artists do it, entertainers and sports figures alike do it, and sometimes those born with a pioneering spirit like Henry Ford, the Wright brothers and Thomas Edison - to name just a few - invent something that changes the way we live.

Then and only then can someone like Stuart Shockley supersede the invisible limitations imposed by an otherwise simple and somewhat paltry existence. In so doing, he not only makes his job easier to perform on a daily basis, he effectively opened up an entire new way of doing business in what would become a speed faster than light. As such, our passions – i.e. our five senses - lead us to embrace that which we feel we must have in order to lead a self-actualized existence. Then so too must our senses conclude he has been wronged in terms of trying to first

legitimize his invention and then reap the
rewards of such a bold discovery.

*

Technology was at its infancy when Stuart
first began his studies at Arkansas College of
Technology learning to be a programmer, but even
so, he saw the potential for good as well as evil
when it came to expanding technology. What he
couldn't possibly have foreseen was how his gift
for technological innovation would change his
life forever, though not necessarily for the
better.

In terms of the five senses, he's been
forced to use all of them in order to simply
survive while constantly building a case against
his detractors. With crystal clear vision, he's
cataloged each incident that might otherwise be
called an anomaly in terms of the typical day-to-
day interactions one expects in a work
environment, from the comings and goings of co-
workers just prior to chemical exposure, to
keeping detailed records of having been tailed by

others outside of work. Even now there is visual evidence to suggest his home has been placed under surveillance and is being monitored by a mysterious new neighbor who only recently relocated here from Dallas about the same time he and I began writing this book.

Running a trace on his license plate revealed the man's name, age, current home ownership in Dallas and the fact he works in technology. On the other hand, Stuart's own visual observations have told him since this new neighbor settled in, he never leaves his home but instead remains sequestered inside with blinds remaining closed regardless of the time of day or current weather. At one point a woman and small children – presumably his family – visited on a weekend, but then departed very quickly without incident.

However, a recent experiment concocted by Stuart and myself over dinner seemed to garner an extreme reaction from the newcomer. Deciding he'd had enough, Stuart took a picture of a neighborhood watch sign and printed it with the intent of placing it underneath his windshield wiper.

Almost instantaneously – and before the printed photo was ever actually placed on his automobile – the young man exited his home and then drove aimlessly throughout the immediate neighborhood, passing by Stuart's home at least three separate times and then up the hill immediately to the south before turning around and returning to his abode. Are the incidents related? It's impossible to say, but it is yet one more anomaly among many.

*

Listening has been another important tool when it came to having fended for himself. Within the course of countless meetings with employers, co-workers, attorneys and people he's never known, Stuart's been over-ruled whenever he sought some form of recognition or compensation for his work, which has led to being fired on two occasions – by the same company – while being baited by numerous others, not to mention having been controlled and manipulated through regular exposure to harmful chemicals both inside the workplace and in apartments he was renting.

Attorneys who have promised him protection under patent laws and satisfaction from having been wronged by partners and former clients alike have either left their posts at prestigious law firms in order to pursue other non-related vocations, relocated out-of-state, or refused to take his case with one of them claiming, "I've only seen one other case like this that no one will touch …", while another shouted false accusations at Stuart and his wife, insisting they immediately leave his office and still another claimed health complications which ultimately led to him tendering his resignation, thus leaving Stuart without formal representation during a critical juncture. Another warned him to 'back off' or he might end up dead, while yet another continues even to this day to dangle the carrot of 'money still being out there' while simultaneously claiming he could help despite his lengthy record of incompetence.

But it hasn't all been negative … there has been encouragement – twice – from state troopers who shared their appreciation and wished him well with regard to future endeavors. There have been numerous comments from people on the fringe who have offered him reassurance in the form of having made declarations about unfolding events they should've known nothing about, like when Stuart once made a statement to the effect, "What am I losing by being here today?" Which was quickly followed by the *oh snap!* response, "What does it matter? You'll get your money from Paul."

Then there is that nagging tie to the Secret Service. Why would someone who claimed to have once been Hillary Clinton's direct aid be interested in Stuart at all? Why did the elusive Mr. Fisak whose current operations are located in Atlanta and Palm Beach, Florida – far from Hot Spring's influence – insist upon obtaining personal information from Stuart and then dangle a coveted downtown location he'd always talked about the following day through yet another stranger? At this point, there have been countless clandestine meetings - all of them brimming with innuendo - while failing to allude to much of anything in particular.

However, it does lead this objective bystander to believe there were offers being placed on the table at specific intervals, each of them saying something to the effect of, "Come join us, and we'll take care of you …" But on the other hand, selling one's soul to the devil is a price some might consider too high and therefore an offer one in fact can refuse.

So once the option of seeking legal representation is removed, the only real course of action is to rely upon yourself and your own wits in order to secure satisfaction. Thus holding onto records and keeping a journal becomes the first and second steps toward writing a tell-all book with the intent of exposing the events and their perpetrators as a means to secure the ultimate satisfaction against one's enemies, the same people who have robbed him blind over the course of the past twenty years.

*

Stuart's sense of smell is what first alerted him to the fact he was being exposed to harmful chemicals. While these chemicals may be invisible to the naked eye, they have nonetheless carried with them a rather distinctive odor. The airborne substances - once combined - induce sort of a one/two punch thereby disabling its intended victim.

Whether Stuart found himself in Eldorado working at *Chemx* or in Little Rock employed by *Club Financial* or while staying in an apartment in both towns over one hundred miles apart, the scent has always been the same … a sweet smell eventually followed by a much stronger, more pungent, bitter aroma that burned his throat and instantly made it difficult to breathe. Depending upon the severity of the attack, he has sometimes been rendered partially disabled for several consecutive days.

Therefore, it has been his sense of smell that has acted as a safeguard in the form of eliciting an evacuation policy that over time has essentially become second nature, thus saving his life up until now. However, there is no insurance policy in place capable of guaranteeing its continued success, and it hardly takes a statistician to tell him odds and the law of averages may be working against him in the long run.

So why not put it out there for the *court of public opinion* to decide damages in this case? While it may be easier to refuse to have an opinion, it certainly isn't safer, because if it can happen to one man, it can happen to anyone, and I for one don't like those odds.

*

Regarding a sense of taste, when one looks at the body of evidence, the resulting impressions leave far more than a bad taste in one's mouth, as Stuart's been forced to rely on the burning effects on his tongue and throat to signal an immediate call to action.

Still I have to wonder what kind of long term effects he may have suffered due to the sheer number of incidences of exposure, or begin to determine the toll such physical and mental stress perpetuated over a period of two decades has taken? In terms of personal injury, damages have been decided with the express intent to punish offenders while discouraging future attempts toward committing the same type of offense.

According to legalmatch.com, *they are mostly awarded in particularly extreme cases where the defendant acted intentionally, or in a way that greatly disregarded the plaintiff's safety.*

Some general guidelines for how to calculate punitive damages include:

- The defendant's actions usually need to be greater than mere negligence. That is, they need to have acted with an obvious disregard for principles of care and safety. An example of this an intentional tort such as assault.

- Punitive damages aren't usually awarded on their own. They are generally issued as an accompaniment to "actual" damages such as compensatory damages (damages that are intended to reimburse the plaintiff for their losses).
- Punitive damages must be "relatively proportionate" to the actual damages award. In most jurisdictions, punitive damages cannot exceed four times the amount of compensatory damages

- See more at:

LaMance, Ken. "How to Calculate Punitive Damages." *LegalMatch*. Legalmatch.com, 8 July 2015. Web.

*

Although there has been no direct physical altercation, there has indeed been a physical assault in terms of continued exposure to hazardous chemicals. However, what I believe resonates even louder is the intent behind such actions, as this is a case that speaks of far greater proportions than simple neglect.

Moreover, fueled by corporate greed and dirty politics, this is a clear example of theft of intellectual property followed by numerous attempts at bribery and a well-orchestrated cover-up involving politicians with ties to organized crime, law enforcement, multiple corporations, and the people they answer to who continue to remain behind the scenes. Their combined actions have led to the systematic deconstruction of a man's life in addition to the possible murder of his own father. So I ask, "Is there an award too great?"

What is now lost is gone forever. So the best anyone can do in such a situation is focus on the future and how compensatory damages along with punitive damages could change Stuart's life going forward, as well as those of his ex-wife and children who were, after all, the most innocent victims in all of this.

Paying a man his worth – even at this late date – would not only change his ability to do right by his family, but also restore his dignity and peace-of-mind, which is ultimately too great to put an actual figure on in terms of the big picture. Even today, Stuart contends his needs are simple. All he's ever wanted is to be paid for his work and to be left in peace.

*

Finally, although it's difficult to place your finger on exactly what's happened with so many pieces of the puzzle still missing, it's not entirely incredible to see something terribly wrong has occurred. There is enough incongruity present in terms of how each of us expects to lead our daily lives both in and outside the workplace to bear closer examination.

Therefore, when one touches upon the evidence as combined with a detailed journal outlining the events as they transpired in real time in conjunction with numerous accounts of 'accidental' brushes with total strangers inexplicably bearing gifts, it doesn't take a genius to fill in some of those blanks. So I ask, using the words of the fictitious character, *Superman*, shouldn't *truth, justice and the American way* still prevail over those who not only fail to understand its meaning, but also seek to destroy its foundation from the inside?

The story behind *Superman* is really an

interesting one as it relates to this modern tale. As articulated on the comic's homepage, I like to think in many ways it is as relevant today as it was back then. Because I prefer to think of the common man - and to be fair, women as well - the one who gets up at the same time every day, gets dressed and goes off to work in hopes of building a better future, as the backbone of our nation.

In the process, they are paying more than their fair share of taxes to help prop up an economy that strives to care for all of us. This is and has always been the American dream, and no one has the right to steal it right out from under us for reasons that are purely selfish. However, it's only by banding together and taking matters into our own hands can any of us hope to triumph over the insidious evil that continues to perpetrate our demise.

*

Superman: Truth, Justice, and the American Way
"Faster than a speeding bullet, more powerful than a locomotive, able

to leap tall buildings in a single bound"

1938 was a dark time for America, crime and economic collapse spread over the land as war loomed in the distance. Men sought diligently for work to support their families, the Mob seized their claws on whatever they could, and in Washington; the President worked long hours repairing the critical state our fractured country was in. Yet, Americans managed to hold firm to hope, setting aside the worries of the day - we found peace of mind and joy at the movies, on the radio, and in the printed page.

Then, two men from Cleveland introduced us to a legend. America would find a renewed hope and strength in their caped icon. The common man didn't feel so small and helpless anymore. Joe Shuster and Jerry Siegal gave the Nation a hero, not from America like Babe Ruth nor of this world like Tarzan; but, a champion from far beyond the stars... from the planet Krypton. I will always picture him standing behind a beam of light, holding the American flag in one hand and the other on his hip, full of pride and determination, as the John Williams theme plays triumphantly.

Grayson, Josh. "Superman: Truth, Justice and the American Way." *SUPERMAN HOMEPAGE*. Supermanhomepage.com, 2000. Web.

*

In conclusion, I am reminded of a statement Cedric Gilson made in his online blog in which he outlined the advantage of drawing a straight line between the law and our five senses. Gilson contended – and I paraphrase – "While one cannot experiment with the law, one can experiment with how the law is applied ...' As a result, no one need be imprisoned by a capitalistic society wherein certain properties like money and power speak the loudest.

By drawing upon our intuition and through the use of certain logic, we the people – once pushed into the proverbial corner - can be stimulated to respond with greater might by simply refusing to idly sit by as if accepting the cards we've been dealt. To quote the words once made famous by actor, Howard Beale, back in 1976 in the film *Network* which were delivered while speaking from the television airwaves, "All I know is that first, you've got to get mad. You've got to say, 'I'm a human being, goddammit! My life has value!'."

He then directs his television audience to get up out of their chairs, go to their windows, open them and hang out their heads and yell, "I'm mad as hell, and I'm not going to take this anymore!"

Thus it's only after having reached your wit's end will justice be served, once the working men and women of this nation unite together while simultaneously demanding what was once rightfully theirs be returned to its proper owner. Then when justice is served and civil liberties reinstated, consumer confidence will return and the expectation for a more equally balanced society will return as well, thereby creating the kind of paradigm shift mankind is in desperate need of right now if it is to survive in any recognizable form. Apocalyptic views of the future will begin to recede into the background the very moment hope is restored and truth once again reigns supreme.

*

OFF THE RECORD: While attending the University of Utah in Salt Lake City as a freshman back in the early 1980's, my political science instructor – a man from Berkley named Joseph Navarro – had his class read a book written by Michael Parenti titled "Democracy for the Few". A scholar from Yale and a political scientist and historian, Mr. Parenti haled from

New York City and wrote about popular subjects of interest. This book – along with brilliant classroom dialogue – changed my entire perspective of the world and politics.

Its unique take on the existence and propagation of an invisible class system carefully crafted and structured within traditional political institutions and those who control them gives the reader a provocative view of American capitalism. Taken to heart, it cannot help but change the way one views politicians, lobbyists and their primary motivation … power.

Perhaps that's why I've been able to use my own vision to form an opinion about Stuart's case, what's happened here and why it continues even today, where others have been more likely to write it off as an example of paranoia due to their complete lack of understanding. Although some might see that as cynicism at its finest, I see it as just the opposite, because I continue to believe there are people who have refused to sell out to a system that would seek to render them powerless. And captured within their refusal are qualities like honor and a willingness to do the right thing.

Some might call that naïve, but I don't think so. However, only time will tell …

Parenti, Michael. "Democracy For The Few, 9th Edition." *Michael Parenti Political Archive.* Michaelparenti.org. Web.

CONCLUSION

When I first began this journey with Stuart
just over two months ago, I wasn't exactly sure
what I thought. After all, ever since I'd known
him, he had always been one of the most laidback
individuals I'd ever associated with on a semi-
regular basis. He'd always been naturally
charming, intelligent, and good-looking. He also
possessed a dry sense-of-humor I really
appreciated. Moreover, he was from a good family
who had instilled within him a high sense of
morality and decency during the course of his
upbringing, characteristics that would follow him
into adulthood, while remaining the driving force

behind a multitude of important decisions yet to come.

However, the man sitting across from me at the bar that first night at the *Colorado Grill* was anything but relaxed. In fact, his demeanor was entirely different from any I'd ever witnessed on previous occasions.

He began by saying, "You know we have a little history …"

To which I replied, "Yes …"

Then he asked, "Did I ever mention anything to you about what was going on?"

Puzzled, I looked back at him as if waiting for some type of explanation.

Then he looked me dead in the eyes and in all seriousness said, "I need to tell you something …" in a leading fashion, while I waited without responding, unsure as to exactly what I should expect.

Then without blinking he said, "I'm gay."

Instantly my mind shot off in a tangent as I replayed moments from a brief history we'd once shared that suggested otherwise. I sat there motionless, unsure what to say as I continued processing his statement. Why was he telling me this? Was he soliciting my support? If so, he had that. It must have been a lengthy pause before I took a breath and began to speak when he burst out laughing. Ahhhh "I'm not gay", there it was, that uncanny wit had at once *gotten me* before the conversation took a decidedly dark turn.

As he poured me a fresh margarita – my first rather quickly consumed – he said, "So you're a writer," to which I shook my head affirmative.

*

The result of that first meeting was nothing I could have prepared myself for in advance, as I witnessed firsthand the once easygoing spirit I'd known since childhood morph into that of a survivor forced to confront numerous opponents – both seen and unseen – in order to simply endure the events of his life. Others who didn't know him like I did might have considered him more than a little bit paranoid – perhaps even delusional – but I didn't. Not for a moment, because beneath this new exterior I could still see the same person I'd always known still thriving, rational, thoughtful and considerate, with a well-developed sense of heightened awareness as to everything going on around him. At once, I gained a new admiration for the man he'd become, knowing just how strong he had to have been in order to hold on to his sanity all these years.

As I drove home that night, I pondered the questions circling through my mind on a continuous loop. Was this something I really want to do? Was this even something I could do? The answers to those questions didn't come to me immediately. I had considerable digging to do through pages upon pages of records while simultaneously consulting with that same inner voice that had served as my own guide when it came to making life-altering decisions.

Eventually I came to envision myself seated before a large table covered with pieces of an intricate jigsaw puzzle spread out before me. As I picked up each piece one-by-one in order to examine it closely before searching for its mate amongst the vast array of possibilities, a picture began to emerge. Much to my chagrin, the image taking shape began telling a story of greed, power and corruption at the highest possible levels.

It was a challenge to complete it. The pieces were many and varied in shape and size - and sometimes the impression was something I didn't even wish to see, because it wreaked havoc with certain core beliefs I'd held dear for most of my adult life.

But as a worshiper of truth, I couldn't look away. I'd already been exposed to a new sense of reality, and all efforts to bury it somewhere deep within the recesses of my own subconscious wasn't going to make it go away. Therefore, writing this story became something of a catharsis for both Stuart and me. As I came to remind him frequently throughout this process, while we cannot change the past, we can at least try and bring about a better future for you, your family and all who have been persecuted for nothing more than having lived their own truth.

"You are a man of strong Christian faith," I said, reminding him on one particularly challenging day, to which he agreed, "Then remember – even in the face of such adversity – Jesus never walked away." He saw it through to the end, and so did we.

*

On the surface, this case looks like so many other shocking, however unremarkable, cases of corporate greed followed up with an unhealthy dose of negligent – even ineffective – legal representation. While that may leave most of us feeling a little unsettled, more than likely it only serves to confirm some of our long-held suspicions about our society in general. However, a much closer examination reveals that while it may have begun as nothing more than just that, at some point it mutated into something far greater

in scope, thereby superseding Arkansas'
boundaries as the ultimate quest for power
reached far greater heights.

Why Stuart Shockley one might ask? Why this
little-known computer programmer from Arkansas?
The simplest answer can be found by asking yet
another question. What do you think the concept
of digital communications was worth at its
inception?

To answer that question, those who are able
must think back to a time somewhere in the mid-
late nineteen nineties when cellular service was
all analog. Mobile telephones were originally *bag
phones* we either had to carry around or wear on
our shoulders like a handbag. Service was spotty
at best, calls were dropped left and right and
roaming charges were at the very minimum price
prohibitive.

Going digital completely revamped an
otherwise marginally effective way of
communicating and then quickly spread across the
entire globe like wildfire. Thus today, we are a

society whose not only become entirely dependent upon the technology we keep, but also a world whose nations are owned and operated by super-computers placed in strategic locations throughout the biosphere. Digital communications has spawned entire new industries like drone surveillance and cyber security, with no foreseeable end in sight to its uses. The possibilities are so endless, it literally boggles the mind.

*

At the time Stuart created *Rattle-Buck*, no one – and I repeat, no one – was doing anything like it. While he may have originally designed this invention with the express intent of utilizing it in the deer woods, all of the components were assembled to communicate digitally from one location to another with increased battery life and the ability to operate the apparatus from a remote location.

In order to make this happen, his research went from schematics to the library where he did considerable background research on companies across the country whose current advances he could utilize and somehow fold into his own. Thus he ended up speaking to a variety of them at length in order to bolster his own knowledge and basic understanding of what he was trying to accomplish. Once there, he took his designs and assembled several prototypes he subsequently tested for accuracy before filing for a patent with the express intention of mass marketing it for profit.

Everything was good up to that point, that is until he hired a patent attorney who then began shopping his invention to others, and before Stuart knew it, people who once greeted him with such enthusiasm, suddenly refused to take his calls while veiled threats with even darker implications began making their way into everyday conversation.

In an instant, it was as if somebody had flipped an invisible switch which effectively took life from something most would recognize as normal to something else far more incendiary in proportion, including constant surveillance and multiple instances of exposure to hazardous chemicals, which rendered him weak and powerless, the effects of which sometimes endured for days at a time. In addition, there has been constant monitoring of his movements from one job position to another for the past nineteen years, to name only a few of the infractions he's been called upon to deal with regularly. As a result, life has been anything but normal.

With the dissolution of his marriage and his children having been severely affected by all of this, not to mention the absence of trust between himself and what was once his closest friends, Stuart has been more or less forced to *go it alone* due to harboring the constant fear of bringing anyone too close. Thus a solitary existence was the only responsible choice he could make in terms of protecting those around him.

He even brought me on board with the

greatest apprehension, making me agree to numerous disclaimers while securing my sincere promise I would bail should anything out of the ordinary begin to surface in my own life. His greatest concern throughout this entire process has always been my safety, which has made me work that much harder to give him some kind of satisfaction.

Thinking back to when my research first commenced, it could have been several things that began this whole ordeal for Stuart and his family, from his having been the first to do away with *IBM's* RPG cycle due to his having combined his knowledge of PS/1, COBOL, Basic and RPG back in '91 and '92. Or it may have been related to Stuart's having written X-MODEM in on AS400, thereby allowing communication directly to PC's. Or the reason might still be buried somewhere in the lawsuit he once had against Paul Lancaster, or more likely it is a combination of *all of the above*. We may never know for sure, but what is the greatest certainty in all of this is that life inexplicably changed the moment he sought to better himself by changing the world.

*

While this may seem like more of a local concern to some in terms of the companies and the people represented in this case, the moment outsiders – like Robert Fisak – began unexpectedly making their way onto the scene, casting the net for possible perpetrators suddenly became a much broader concept. The direct involvement of Secret Service – especially one who claimed to have ties to the Clintons – suddenly took this case of theft and subsequent abuse to a national, albeit global proportion, which makes sense when one considers how well orchestrated the crimes against Stuart have been, as well as how difficult it is to get a straight answer from anyone either directly or indirectly involved.

As I've stated often throughout this manuscript, whether in the form of a bribe or ominous warnings to essentially *back off*, innuendo has become the norm and not the exception. Had Stuart accepted what I believe was to have been some form of inducement at the pizza parlor from his co-worker at *Club Financial*, all of this might have been over years ago, while on the other hand, had he continued working for *Chemx* down in Eldorado, he might very well be dead.

Through it all, Stuart has refused to sell his soul, and he has suffered greatly in the process, whether that be in relation to the subsequent loss of his family or the inability to lead a peaceful existence, which is why his story should matter to anyone who values intangibles like hard work, honesty and justice in terms of the *American Way*.

It is my belief that turning a deaf ear while refusing to see the ugliness at play threatens the very foundation of the freedom we all hold so dear. From the beginning, our ancestors braved months on the high seas crossing the Atlantic enduring famine, pestilence and disease for the hope of a better life in a brave new land free of the kind of tyranny and oppression incumbent within a hierarchal existence. Therefore, to withhold justice in this matter – in a sense – equates to saying their sacrifices didn't matter and leaves the door wide open for the same people to go on harming others.

*

While I believe in politics there has always been a need to consider the common good over the desires of just a few, I can't help believing those who reside at the top tier of Capitalism have – in their ongoing quest for power – somehow lost sight of that fact, essentially flopping the balance of power in favor of their needs, wants and desires as opposed to governing the masses. Thus we fall victim as a result of those cutting deals in groups far away from public scrutiny or approval. Is this the world any of us wants?

While secret societies like the *Illuminati* and *The Bilderberg Group* may have originated with the purest principle based upon the concept of a world order designed not only to protect those at the top, but also to provide for those of us who work for them, I can't help believing that much power assembled under one roof can't help but breed corruption. As a result, corruption cannot help but collapse under its own weight.

Therefore, maybe it's high time the masses unite in a manner capable of rising above the petty differences associated with things like party affiliation and take a deeper look at the big picture - which is freedom - and something both our ancestors as well as the brave men and women who have worn military uniforms have fought and died protecting. Maybe then we will find the necessary strength in numbers capable of ridding ourselves of the kind of *secrets* that threaten to destroy us from within.

At some point, everyone either has or knows someone who has felt powerless within our current system of government. So why not take it back? It doesn't necessitate a revolution. By demanding more from those who govern while insisting upon greater accountability from our leadership - not to mention transparency – we can begin to restore our faith in society and the common good. Isn't that the kind of nation we all idealize?

I used to believe in the two-party system, but now I'm not so sure. It seems to have created the kind of divide that benefits no one. Why not instead just have candidates united under one umbrella that is America, land of the free, home of the brave? Then once again democracy would reign supreme.

Then showing up at the poles in record numbers while insisting upon candidates whose ideology resonates across the land would begin the kind of change we could all adapt to, as we braced ourselves for the kind of new world order designed with the people in mind. Concepts like *for the people, by the people* would no longer be that of a historical reference, but rather a way of life we could each be happy to call our own.

*

Therefore, when I suggest justice for Stuart Shockley and his family, in a much broader sense I'm proposing we find those capable of stealing a man's intellectual property - and by extension, his life - and then auctioning it off to the highest bidder in exchange for political favors, *guilty as charged*. It's only by making someone pay in a way designed to *send a message* do we hope to protect ourselves from the same type of threat going forward.

From the onset, when I considered the risk/reward potential I might be opening myself up to if I decided to take on this new project, the rewards far outweighed the risk. As such, I can't help believing that's a good indicator for all of us when it comes to answering the age old question, "Am I doing the right thing?"

What about you?

OFF THE RECORD: Following is an excerpt posted online by "The Washington Post" which has since been updated:

Before Monica Lewinsky, there was Whitewater.

The impeachment report that Kenneth Starr delivered to the House in September 1998 was the product of only one of many lines of inquiry the independent counsel has pursued in more than four years of probing the president.

Originally appointed to investigate a failed Arkansas real estate deal involving the Clintons almost 20 years ago, Starr's scope expanded over time to include a bewildering range of accusations of fraud, obstruction of justice and abuse of power allegedly involving President Clinton and the first lady, as well as some of their closest friends and advisers.

Froomkin, Dan. "Untangling Whitewater." *Washingtonpost.com Staff.* Washingtonpost.com, 2000. Web.

Therefore, it's no wonder Stuart – being an Arkansan – decided to travel there as well, if for nothing more than to see what all the fuss was about. As such, he decided to bottle the famed water and offer it for sell as a novelty. However, at this point, I can't help wondering if it doesn't possess far greater significance in how the events of Stuart's life have unfolded during the course of the past twenty years.

Exhibit V. Although the image is a little grainy, as digital photography wasn't available at that time, back in 1994 all intriguing roads in Arkansas seemed to lead to one destination … White Water.

Exhibit X. for reference, following is Stuart's Professional Resume'

DATE	COMPANY	PROGRAMS
1981 – 1984	Ben Hogan Construction	S34
1984 – 1986	Koppers Inc	S36
1986 – 1989	Computer Data Services	S36/AS400
1989 – 1991	Lavender & Wyatt	AS400 RPG 4 ***
1991 – 1996	Self-Employed	S36/AS400 RPG II, IV
1996	Chemx	AS400 ILE
1996 – 1997	Club Financial	AS400 ILE
1997 – 1998	Bartman Systems	AS400 ILE
1999 – 2000	Pleasure Arts	AS400 ILE
2000	NetSource	AS400 ILE
2002 – 2015	MedCollect	AS400 ILE

An Important Note … since the submission of his letter to Mary Safford – his direct supervisor at MedCollect - dated 07/09/15 Stuart had not experienced any further on-the-job incidents until very recently. However, as our work neared completion, exposure began again.

Exhibit W. Going forward, the following picture represents a potentially damning piece of evidence …. This is Stuart's current desk at work there at MedCollect. This photo shows not only the date and time - as noted on his computer screen - but also the letter he'd given his direct supervisor, Mary Safford (see Exhibit C & D. on pages 125-127), protesting his continued exposure to dangerous chemicals in the workplace, as well as the air filter he collected from his office in order to have tested at an independent lab ….

... *RESULTS PENDING.*

REFERENCES

WEBSITES

- IBM Highlights 1985 – 1989 PDF. (n.d.). 23

- Lwsi.com. (n.d.). 29

- Davis, MD Phd, Charles Patrick. "Hemoglobin Levels." *EMedicineHealth.* Emedicinehealth.com, 12 Nov. 2014. Web. 116

- "How Workplace Chemicals Enter the Body, OSH Answers Factsheet." *Canadian Centre for Occupational Health and Safety.* Ccohs.ca, 1 Apr. 2009. Web. 120

- "Safety Data Sheet, R-1150 Ethylene." *National Refrigerants, Inc.* Refrigerants.com/pdf, 1 Apr. 2015. Web. 122

- Morris, Roger. "Stories of Bill, Interview." *Frontline.* PBS.org. Web. 13 June 1996. 149

- Harklute, Aurora. *"Signs of Asphyxiation."* Livestrong, 24 October 2013. 193

- "The XXXXXX Group to Establish E-Solutions Development Center in XXXXXX ; Center Expected to Add 250 Technical Jobs Over Next Two Years." *PR Newswire.* Web. 207

- "Deltic Home Page." *Deltic.com.* Web. 228

- "Undersea Recovery Group Corp (UNDR:OTC US)." *Executive Profile* Robert A. Fisak. Bloomberg Business. Web. 255

- "Gang-Stalking and Electronic Mind Control Community Spreads." *Atlanta.cbs.local.com,* 17 May 2014. Web. 264

- "250 Case Torture From Europe." *To You Our Selected Witnesses.* Docslide.us. Web. 267

- "Doctors Who Believe in Gang Stalking." *Gang Stalking.* KIWIPEDIA The Honest Encyclopedia. Web. 271

- "Acenaphthylene." Chemistry Learner. Web. 275

- Frater, Jamie. "Top Ten Secret Societies." *Listverse.com.* 27 Aug. 2007. Web. 297

- Stone, Jon. "4 Things We Know about the Secretive Bilderberg Group and 1 Thing We'll Never Know." *Independent.co.uk.* Independent, 9 June 2015. Web. 302

- Lendman, Stephen. "The True Story of the Bilderberg Group" and What They May Be Planning Now, A Review of Daniel Estulin's Book." *Globalresearch.ca.* Global Research, 25 May 2014. Web. 303

- Watson, Steve. "BILDERBERG BACKS HILLARY FOR 2016 PRESIDENCY Chief Hillary Advisor to Attend Secret Confab." *ALEX JONES' INFOWARS.COM BECAUSE THERE IS A WAR ON FOR YOUR MIND.* Infowars.com, 8 June 2015. Web. 308

- Gilson, Cedric. "Law and the Senses: Symposium, Performance, Phenomenome?" *Critical Legal Thinking – Law & the Political -* . Criticallegalthinking.com, 25 June 2013. Web. 313

- LaMance, Ken. "How to Calculate Punitive Damages." *LegalMatch.* Legalmatch.com, 8 July 2015. Web. 327

- Grayson, Josh. "Superman: Truth, Justice and the American Way." *SUPERMAN HOMEPAGE.* Supermanhomepage.com, 2000. Web. 331

- Parenti, Michael. "Democracy For The Few, 9th Edition." *Michael Parenti Political Archive.* Michaelparenti.org. Web. 335

- Froomkin, Dan. "Untangling Whitewater." *Washingtonpost.com Staff.* Washingtonpost.com, 2000. Web. 353

EXHIBITS

- Exhibit A – Original programming notes from Stuart's handwritten journal - 30

- Exhibit B – Note copied and pasted from Stuart's journal re: chemical exposure - 115

- Exhibit C – Documentation of exposure covering an 11 month period - 125

- Exhibit D – Letter submitted to current employer re: chemical exposure - 126

- Exhibit E – Journal notes re: years of persecution - 149

- Exhibit F – Letter to RJ Brown dated 5/26/98 - 164

- Exhibit G – Letter to RJ Brown dated 6/26/98 - 166

- Exhibit H – Letter to RJ Brown dated 8/04/98 - 168

- Exhibits H1 & H2 – From Stuart's handwritten notes re: RJ Brown/Paul Lancaster – 170 &171

- Exhibit I – Letter to Judge Hearnsberger dated 9/28/98 appealing for information -171

- Exhibit J – Letter to Judge Hearnsberger dated 10/8/98 re: intellectual property – 209 – 212

- Exhibit K – Letter to RJ Brown dated 9/17/98 – 212 – 216

- Exhibit L – Letter *To Whom It May Concern* re: final appeal - 241

ADDITIONAL IMAGES

About the Authors

Joyce formerly worked as a professional interior designer in excess of 25 years spearheading projects both nationally and abroad, while simultaneously cultivating an audience for her writing through several book publications and a successful online blog. Though no stranger to real life portrayals intended to enrich the lives of her readers, this is her first effort at writing a true story based entirely upon the life of another. She attended Texas Christian University and is currently residing in Hot Springs, Arkansas to be near her family.

Stuart has dedicated his adult life to streamlining processes while constantly developing and refining new software programs enabling the companies he's worked for to reach new heights in the business world. His knack for innovation combined with a spirit for invention led him to design a device to utilize digital technology which could be operated from a remote location. He originally attended Ouachita Baptist University and then went on to learn programming at Arkansas College of Technology. He resides in Hot Springs, Arkansas.

Social Media

Be the First to Hear

about News & Updates

from

Trust but Verify

A Great Injustice

Follow us on

Email: *trustbverify88@gmail.com*

Facebook: *www.facebook.com/tbverify*

www.ingramcontent.com/pod-product-compliance
Lightning Source LLC
Chambersburg PA
CBHW030417290526
45786CB00001B/21